T0368356

# *beyond* FREEDOM

## THE DIARY OF AN IRANIAN GIRL

### SARAH TEHRANI

authorHOUSE®

*AuthorHouse™*
*1663 Liberty Drive*
*Bloomington, IN 47403*
*www.authorhouse.com*
*Phone: 833-262-8899*

*Published by AuthorHouse  11/15/2024*

*ISBN: 979-8-8230-3757-0 (sc)*
*ISBN: 979-8-8230-3756-3 (e)*

*Library of Congress Control Number: 2024923813*

*Print information available on the last page.*

*This book is based on actual events and a true story. The author has taken the liberty to modify names, places, events, and people to protect their identities, while maintaining the essence of what truly happened. While she has used creative freedom to expand on the story as thoughshe were reliving it, the core elements and events are all true.*

*Editor: Kristin Campbell at C&D Editing*

# CONTENTS

## Part III: Escape, Freedom, Stress, and Prison

## Part IV: One Last Time

## Part V: New Beginnings

## Part VI: Another Man in My Life

# A PERSONAL NOTE OF THANKS

To all the people who taught me the truth, were unfailingly kind to me, and helped me understand life better.

To my late father, who made every effort to support me, who shared his knowledge and experiences and all he had learned in life with me, whether I was prepared to listen and learn or not. Above all else, he gave me a better insight into living my life.

To my late mother, who taught me to choose the right path and way of living and had faith in me, even when I was lacking it in myself. She was my role model for patience.

To my dear grandparents, who were a role model for many people, including me. Their life story has always inspired me, as they were the true definition of love.

To my two brothers, who have been my rock and helped me through difficult times on many occasions. I love them with all my heart.

To friends who have accepted me despite my mistakes and who were always there when I needed them. Their friendships have taught me great lessons about myself with the honesty and love they offer.

And to my partner in life, who chose to share his life with me and who has always been by my side on the ride, whether rocky or smooth.

# INTRODUCTION

I would like to share my life story in Iran, as far as I remember it. It's true that you change and grow in life, but it is my dream to share what I experienced as a teenager. I believe it might provide insight to many of those living in that country and other parts of the world, especially the young girls who need to know they are not alone and that life is not limited on how they might experience it in youth.

There is much more to see, learn, and experience in the world. People interested in knowing more about Iran and the lifestyle of people living there during the past forty years might benefit from this book, too. It is the real-life story of a girl who grew up in the northern part of Tehran … and is exactly as old as the 1979 revolution!

That girl is me!

# PART I

## The Beginning of the End

# CHAPTER 1

## The End Feels Good

### *Two Missing Days*

A mysterious 19-year-old girl lay in the ambulance as it made its way through the bustling streets of Tehran, the blaring sirens cutting through the night. I remained unconscious, my parents by my side, their faces etched with worry and uncertainty. My identity and the events leading up to my current state remained an enigmatic puzzle waiting to be unraveled. Just a few hours ago, I, alongside my two friends, had been on our way back to Tehran after a trip up north. Over the past few days, I had been devastated by her breakup with Abtin, my boyfriend of 2 years. But no one could have guessed I could meet with an accident. I was driving the car so I could distract myself from overwhelming thoughts of the breakup, but my depression was having a firm grip on me. While driving the car, I had a momentary blackout, which prompted the car to lose balance and hit the pavement. Although my friends were okay as they didn't sustain any grieving injury, I was unwell and injured.

I had not been feeling well, so I asked my parents if I could stay at my best friend, Maryam's house, for a few days. Maryam's sister, Ana, was also going through a series of breakups with her boyfriend. I didn't feel lonely when I and Maryam were together. We had talked all night about their shared experiences.

Ana had persisted to her parents that Ana and her boyfriend to get married and so they can to continue their relationship. Ana was only twenty; she wasn't ready to get married, nor was her boyfriend. Therefore, there was so much drama.

On the other hand, my parents wouldn't let me to get married at that age. My father always said jokingly, "She must never marry."

My mom, however, would smile and say, "You can't ever say never!"

She would also tell me, "When the time comes, you will know if it's the right thing to do." Neither of them would ever suggest anything that would push me to think of marriage.

This attitude was not common in families with young girls at that time. Although it has changed a lot from the time when there were arranged marriages, many families would suggest or even push their daughters to consider marrying a specific person or have goals for their daughters' weddings from a young age. That usually came with the perspective of someone who is known by parents and meets their standards, whether wealth, education, or being acquainted.

I was highly depressed and had been feeling so bad about everything that I didn't even want to get up and wasn't motivated to do anything. My friends talked to me so much and told me to be positive, but no one else could feel he pain that I felt inside.

My relationship with Abtin had become my whole life. It had given me hope that I might live my dream—being closer to freedom. I wanted to be away from school and university, the misery that I felt, the loneliness at home, not being close to my parents, and fighting with my younger brother, my strict father, and my always worried mother. I didn't even feel close to Maryam, my best friend anymore.

Why did life have to be so bitter?

This time, Abtin had really broken up with me and had said there wouldn't be a way back. It felt like all I had built up over the past 2 years was falling apart.

I had hoped this relationship would end up in marriage, like some of her other friends who were getting married at about the same age. Little did I know that most of these marriages wouldn't survive. Some of my friends had made the wrong choices. Some had been forced to marry by their parents and the pressure of their culture. I didn't realize at the time that this would end up impacting them for the rest of their lives.

A girl who got married at around 20 most likely was not ready to start a proper marriage. That was the way our grandmothers had lived. They had gotten married early back then when life was so different. It was not right in this era, with life being so complicated, with so many choices … countries being a few hours flights from each other, people living in mixed cultures, and so on.

The north of the country was beautiful, as always. To get there from Tehran, you had to take one of the three roads that went over the high Alborz Mountain. On the way, I felt refreshed. I have always enjoyed watching the beautiful mountain forest that is connected to the sea.

People who live in Tehran go to this seaside area for vacation. The natural beauty is extraordinary. The forest meets the sea in some parts, and the beaches are beautiful and sandy. Many people have great memories of their holidays in the northern part, Shomal, which means *"the north"* in Farsi.

We listened to music and had fun on the road. I started to forget my sorrow and the negative feelings that seemed to suffocate me.

The smell of fresh raw rice was so aromatic it could make you drunk. Then, as soon as we drove down from the top of the mountain toward the sea, it started. The closer they got to the sea, the smell of the sea mixed with the humidity in the air was so refreshing, and the green land around me made me feel so much better.

We arrived at their friend's villa and took our stuff inside the house. We got some rest and then went for a walk. That night, we went to sleep early, and then our other two friends came to visit them the next day.

Once in a while, I remembered the shock of my breakup, and it saddened me deeply. Loneliness was the feeling that bothered me the most, and I had no motivation for the future. Regardless, I kept forcing myself to forget. Being around friends was fun … yet I felt the emptiness. I was bored, but with friends, I had less time to think about what had happened. After all, this was a disaster—him walking out on me so easily. Weren't we meant to be together forever?

I knew I didn't even love him that much, but the concept of him being my first serious boyfriend had strong implications. 2 years of relationship in my 19 years of life was a long time. It was just too difficult to digest that it could be possible for the relationship to end so easily.

The two friends who were visiting us joked and laughed, and it looked like everybody was enjoying themselves … except me.

On the second day, we got busy preparing a barbecue for lunch. We had our lunch and hung out together. I felt restless and low, but, on the other hand, thinking about going back made me anxious. I didn't know why. Maybe I just didn't want to face the reality. I knew I couldn't accept what had happened and was unable to move on.

The next day, Maryam and I packed up and prepared to go back. We helped clean the villa and put everything into the car.

On the way back, the local shops on either side of the road were so colorful in the middle of the green hills and the blue Caspian Sea. The sharp colors of handicrafts, mixed with local food, fresh fish, and fruit in the farmers' market, produced such a live atmosphere.

We stopped on the side of the road to buy jam and cookies. I also got some for my mom, reminding me I didn't feel close to anyone at home. Not my mom, not my dad, not my brothers. My grandparents were really kind to me, but it had been a long time since I had opened up to them. They all felt like strangers. My mom was always there for me if I wanted to talk, but maybe if our relationship was closer, or she could feel my pain like a friend, that would have helped.

I envied Maryam, as she was close to her mom. Maryam's mom always praised her, no matter what she went through. When Maryam and her sister were getting ready to go out, she would admire them and say how beautiful they looked. On the other hand, my mom was always too busy with my brothers, life, and my grandparents. I couldn't blame her for that. I also had my own problems in life, which included my own dad.

My dad was too busy with work, and he was strict at home. I knew my mom would tell him all about my relationship, but I barely had conversations with dad about my personal life openly. We would only have long conversations if there was something to blame me for or if there was something my parents were not happy about. That was when my dad would lecture me for *hours*.

I hated that the most—those long hours of lectures. Even though he was showing me right from wrong and helping me choose the right path long-term, I needed emotional support. I needed a strong support system.

Being close to my parents was something that was missing in my life. I was blocking myself away, too.

I never felt close to my dad until later, because I was always afraid of him or of making him angry. I stopped feeling close to my mom when I was a teenager, as I felt my mom would share all my secrets with my dad. That would only give him a reason to get mad at me or be more strict about going out, having a boyfriend, going skiing, and proceeding with my school studies.

My support system showed me boundaries all the time, but it was not emotionally fulfilling.

There was a deep hole in my soul, being 19 and feeling so alone. At school and at home, everyone was an enemy, and now that my boyfriend was becoming a stranger to me, this was too much to accept.

Was life supposed to be this cruel? Wasn't life meant to be kinder, nicer, and friendlier? Why did everything seem to be so hard? Why was there so much stress that I had to bear? I couldn't understand.

The farther we got from the road on top of the mountains to Tehran, the worse I felt. That severe anxiety and the feeling of sorrow or shock were coming back. That shallow feeling!

I wasn't looking forward to anything in Tehran. Not my university classes or the mountainous town where it was located. Not being at home with all the rules and regulations. A dad who always lectured me and was mostly angry. A mom who was so busy and desperate at times, and not my friend whom I could trust, although I talked to her. Not meeting with friends. Not hanging out with anybody. Even Maryam felt distanced from me, as she didn't understand everything. Nothing could excite me. *He* was out of my life. It seemed like it was the end of everything.

We stopped the car at the holy ground, and I looked around in confusion until Ana turned around and told me, "I want to donate some money."

I also thought of doing the same. "Me, too."

I threw all the money I had in the charity box located at the Imam's shrine.

When we got back to the car, we didn't talk much. It was like none of us felt really happy going back to Tehran. Maryam and Ana were sitting in the front, and I was in the back, making me feel even more alone and sinking back into thoughts.

How could he do this to me? We used to argue and fight, and then I would break up with him, but after a couple of days, I would always call, and we got back together.

This time, however, he had been adamant that he didn't want to get back together anymore. I couldn't understand why. The fact that we were intimate meant so much to me.

I craved a deeper connection. I didn't think about getting married soon, but a breakup had been the last thing on my mind. He was planning to leave the country for good, but he hadn't shared anything with me about being so sure of leaving the country. What about me? I kept thinking to myself. Where was I in his plans? Where did I fit into his future? Was I even there, or was it all just for me and not for him? The more I thought about it, the more restless I felt from the inside.

I wasn't able to digest the fact that a relationship could end like this. The past couple of weeks had been a nightmare. I had even gotten sick with the flu and had gotten so weak that I had stayed in the hospital for a night. Maryam had called Abtin and told him what was going on. He had come to visit me, but all I could witness was his coldness more than his concern. He told me everything was over.

Why? I kept thinking over and over again! How can he be so cruel? How can he do this to me? I don't want to be in this world anymore. How can I stop living?

Sitting in the back of the car, I told my friends, "I feel tired, guys. I'm going to take a nap until we arrive."

"Okay," They responded, glancing at me with concern before looking back at the road.

When I couldn't get enough rest, I asked Maryam if I could drive the car instead.

"But are you okay? Can you drive?" She asked.

"Yes, of course!" I replied.

Then Maryam got to the back of the car, while I sat behind the steering wheel and started driving. I thought the antidepressants weren't doing well, as I still felt depressed. Driving the car was my only option that could distract me for a while.

Before this trip, my mother had taken me to a therapist so I could talk about the breakup and how I felt about it. I told the therapist this was my first serious relationship. The psychiatrist had prescribed anti-depressant pills and advised my parents to watch me for some time. That was it! It was as if nobody could understand my pain, the loneliness, and the heaviness of my heart. It was like a failure, which I wasn't used to. I was definitely not used to failure.

Before driving the car, I had taken few antidepressant pills. The closer we got to Tehran, the worse my feeling of loneliness got.

I was already feeling dizzy …

I couldn't remember anything else until we were in the ambulance, and I saw the shadows of my parents, Maryam's, and Ana's faces, all of whom were scared and some in tears.

The numbness felt good. It was a relief from all the extreme pain that I had borne for years. It was lighter than the heavy burden of being a good girl with all those limitations at school, in society, and even at home: the taboos, the stress of being right or wrong, the question that I could never find an answer to. Shouldn't I be free and happy as a human? This was a getaway, a relief from all the pain.

The first hospital rejected us because they didn't have the facilities. They sent us to another hospital, I didn't remember anything after that.

I woke up with the tubes in my nose, feeling uncomfortable, as though I had experienced shocks and a seizure. I never got to ask my parents whether I had a seizure or if they had given me shocks to wake me up.

A long time after this, my dad mentioned jokingly how silly and immature it was for me to do this. I agreed with my dad, but it would always make me feel uncomfortable to remember and talk about it.

Even though I had woken up, I continued to move between consciousness and unconsciousness, which took me back to silence again and again.

After a really long silence, I woke up dizzy and feeling numb. I couldn't remember where I was. I was wearing a white hospital gown, but the place was unknown to me, and I had to go to the bathroom.

I looked around and tried to get out of the bed. "What day is it?" I asked a girl who was sitting in a chair in the hospital corridor.

"It's Wednesday," the girl replied.

I started walking toward the bathroom with clouds in my brain. I remembered getting back on the road. Maryam had been driving. That was Monday night. Had I slept for two nights?

I remembered I couldn't take it anymore. Life without him was meaningless, and I didn't want to continue.

I turned back to the room. My mother was there, waiting. I was happy to see my mom.

"Hi, Mom."

My mother hugged me. "Sarah Jan, are you feeling okay?"

"Yes, Mom, I'm good," I replied in a low tone.

"Are we going to leave?" I asked.

"We are, dear," My mother replied kindly before continuing, "I'm waiting for the nurse to bring the paperwork and your clothes."

The nurse arrived soon after, smiled at me, and said, "You look much better than before, dear. You'll be fine very soon. Drink a lot of water."

I still wasn't completely all right, but I felt much better, for sure. I also felt … lighter, somehow.

We left the hospital and drove toward our house, which was far away, on the other side of the town.

"Maryam wants you to stay with her for a few days. If you like, you can go there," My mother asked me. mother told her.

I smiled. "Great! I just need to get some of my clothes. Will you drop me off there then, please?" I requested.

My mom seemed calm and kind. She wasn't blaming me and didn't seem upset by my behavior or pissed off, like most of the other times when there had been problems.

She had a calm, quiet, and kind face as if she had completely transformed into a different person. I was still sleepy, but I could recognize the change in my mother. Perhaps everyone now realized how painful everything had become in my young mind. That was what I wanted— for them to understand me.

Selfishly, however, I didn't really care about anything else, not even the danger I had put my life in and what I had put her family through. I still wasn't ready to face my dad—the stress of meeting with him and being in the same place as him at home was overwhelming. Maryam's house would be a much different atmosphere.

"Are you sure?" My mother asked. "Would you be more comfortable there?"

"Yes, I am sure."

"How are you feeling?" Mom asked with concern, reflecting through her expressions.

"Okay, Mom, I promise. Just a little dizzy." I replied.

We didn't talk anymore until we got to Maryam's house.

"Bye, Mom."

With that, I got out of the car, ran up to the house, and rang the bell. Then Maryam opened the door, and we went inside.

What was interesting was the pain of the breakup was gone! I no longer felt the burden. Why? I didn't know, but it was as if I didn't care, or maybe it felt like it had happened a long time ago. There was no pain in my heart, and I didn't feel that bitter loneliness like I had before. I didn't even care about Abtin. I wasn't sure how, but I felt lighter and calmer than I had in a long time.

# CHAPTER 2

# A Little Girl with Big Dreams

As I drifted in and out of my past, the memories of my childhood began to surface. I found myself lost in a reverie, recollecting the moments that shaped me into the person I had become. It was as if the walls of time had dissolved, allowing me to traverse back to the innocence and simplicity of her my youth.

## *Life with My Grandparents*

As a little girl, I used to have short, brunette hair that delicately framed my round lively face. Slender and full of energy, I moved with a graceful vigor that seemed to pulse with life. My bright blue eyes mirrored my insatiable curiosity and enthusiasm for the world. Despite my petite stature, I carried myself with a powerful aura, captivating those around me and drawing them into my vibrant world.

I was constantly at my grandparents' house until I turned nine years old, and we moved to another part of the town. They lived right across from us and had a big yard with a swimming pool. Our houses were located in the north-central part of Tehran, in an area called Mirdamad.

My grandparents' house was like my kingdom, which was extremely different from our own house, where I could get quite tense every now and then due to my parents' disagreements and arguments. I found my dad's severe anger scary, especially because, most of the time, it ended with my mother crying.

My grandparents' place was full of love and freedom. It was where I could spend hours in peace without being stopped or disciplined. It felt like it was my own world, and I was the ruler.

Their big yard was my garden, where I would take care of the plants. The beautiful pool was an ocean, where I would jump in and swim in the afternoons. Whenever my uncle, aunt, and cousins were around, we played in the pool for hours. Then we were given delicious melon slices, prepared by Grandma, which was the best treat after so much jumping up and down and swimming in the water.

I always felt so much love and attention there. My dad believed I got spoiled spending so much time at their house, with them listening to me too much.

Before sunset, all the family—my parents, uncle and aunt, cousins, and grandparents—would gather on the porch, and Grandpa would water the plants. The fresh smell of watered

Plants and soil mixed with jasmine flowers are still in my head today. It reminds me of those beautiful afternoons. The sunset's sunbeams were still warm. Everybody was happy, joking, laughing, and talking about their day.

Grandma was going around like a flying fairy, asking all the kids what they wanted to eat or giving them presents to make sure everybody was happy.

They had five grandchildren back then, all boys but me. I was the first grandchild and the only girl. I was the favorite and definitely spoiled. Their pure love was unconditional, and there was no anger involved.

My grandpa was an ex-military colonel who was honored that he had served in the Shah's regime before the revolution. He was also a national champion in javelin throw two years in a row. He took pride in having shaken hands with the late Shah twenty-four times.

Everything was quite disciplined in my grandparents' house. They used to wake up at six a.m., were seated for lunch by 11:45 a.m., and would start eating by noon.

My grandpa used to tell me stories from when he was young, such as how belief in God and being a good person always helped him in life. He wrote in my first diary book, "*Hope you learn how to make yourself become successful in life.*" I was nine years old when he wrote that, and I couldn't really understand what he meant by "make yourself," but he made me think about it a lot. Those words always stuck with me throughout life.

He used to read Hafiz, a Persian lyric poet, or Khaiam, a polymath known for his contributions to mathematics, astronomy, philosophy, and Persian poetry, with a really nice tone and sound. Then, he would interpret the meanings if I asked a question. He always had to start with a couple of sentences praising Hafiz, and then I would ask him to answer my question. I will never forget how energizing those afternoons were, spending time with my grandparents, and how Grandpa changed my mood when I was upset about something. He always put me in a happy mood, filled with energy and hope. Meanwhile, he was talking about self-belief and how the love of God always guided him to become a national champion when he didn't have anyone to rely on.

His parents had divorced. His dad, who was a well-known architect, had remarried and moved from Isfahan, where he had been born, to another town called Ahvaz in the southern part of Iran. He was the eldest child and mentored his brother, Rami, who was two years younger. He helped Rami to become athletic and encouraged him to participate in competitions when he joined the military university and started his career in the army with the sole intention of helping people to make the world a better place.

He always said he never abused his relationships or power to his own benefit. He was a great horse rider and athlete. Money was not a priority in his life, and he believed in self-growth and spirituality.

He said to me once, "I was alone. I didn't have anyone to support me. My mother was a single mom with many issues to handle, and my younger brother needed support. But I had God, who walked in front of me and showed me the way. When I needed an answer, I just asked Him to answer, and He did."

In my youth, I used to listen to him, stare, and try to understand what he said. Even though I was so little, his words were so powerful that I always remember them. At the time, I used to ask my mom a hundred questions afterward to figure out what he was really referring to.

Grandma and Grandpa were second cousins who had fallen in love when Grandpa was in military university and my grandma was seventeen. He had given her a ring and asked her to marry him. Later on, Grandpa's mother asked her to give the ring back, as she didn't agree with their marriage. But Grandma refused and told her that if he wanted the ring back, he had to ask himself.

They got married and moved out of their hometown of Isfahan, where they lived in different towns where Grandpa had missions throughout his army service. They finally settled in Tehran many years ago and had three kids. They were the definition of love after forty years of marriage.

Grandma's dad had died when she was young, and her mother had raised three children by herself, working as a tailor throughout her hard life.

I hardly ever saw Grandma without a smile on her face. She was the most positive and giving woman whom I have ever known. She hardly ever complained or got upset with others, and her biggest wish was to make us happy.

She adored me! Apart from the love of my parents, it was largely her unconditional love that helped me through many stages of my life. I will always remember her kind words and her passion to see me happy and successful.

She had been married to my grandpa for many years during that time, and they lived together for seventy years before they left this world, only four months apart.

Grandma's kitchen was heaven. It was a big, old kitchen which, to me, seeing it from my short height, was a place where all the magic happened. I was the same height as the oven then, and everything looked bigger and taller from down there.

Her food was delicious, and she made the most aromatic Persian stews and rice that you could imagine. Any food you asked her for, she would make with love.

After lunch, there was naptime for an hour, exactly from 12:45 to 1:45 p.m. I don't ever remember Grandpa missing the two o'clock news. It was as if it was compulsory to listen to the radio at that time.

After the news, Grandpa used to do a card puzzle that he called the Napoléon, or clock puzzle. I would sit next to him, wondering and trying to learn how to solve the puzzle. Sometimes, he played cards with me, too, and let me win intentionally. He would play dumb and say, "What? Are you winning again?" I used to believe him, and I had so much fun. Their house was my kingdom. I played and explored their backyard happily every day with my aunt's cat and other garden creatures, flowers, and leaves. I used to play mostly alone. I would take a doormat into the yard between flowers and trees and make "food" out of leaves and flowers, inviting my imaginary friends for dinner. Sometimes, insects were my playmates, like ants or rolliepollies. I loved nature and being there. It felt so good and free.

They had a patio that felt like a forest to me. The end of it always felt pristine and unspoiled, as the plants were fully grown and too high for me to get there. Lizards always hung out on the patio, too, and it really scared me to see one on the wall, so I would avoid going too near the end of the patio, sticking to the front area so I could run back into the house if anything scared me.

One afternoon, during a weekend, my cousins and second cousins were all playing in the beautifully manicured yard. There were lots of little lights in the garden that made it bright. We were doing all sorts of things, from hide-and-seek to many other games. There were about seven of us, including me and a second cousin who was a boy older than all of us.

At first, we hunted slugs and put them against the hot lights on the ground with sticks in them. The poor slugs melted. It was the cruelest thing I've knowingly done until this day!

Later, I got a freezer bag from Grandma and started collecting rollie pollies. I collected a full bag of them. They weren't moving in the bag when I took it into Grandma's closet and hid it. Little did I know that the rollie pollies would come out of the bag that wasn't even tied up!

In the middle of the night, my grandma started screaming. She was scared to see all those creatures crawling out of her closet. She then woke me up, asking, "What have you done? What are these things in my closet?" I got severely told off for what I had done.

A couple of times, my grandma bought me little yellow chickens that I used to keep there. I made them a house from cardboard and gave them water to drink and seeds to eat. It was really fun to feed them and take care of them. But, after a while, they got sick, and there was little we could do to rescue them.

My grandma was always waiting for me to wish for something, and then she'd make it happen.

Grandpa taught me how to swim and ride a bicycle. He talked about life's lessons often, how the love of God, beliefs, and courage can lead to great achievements. Later in life, this helped me push through difficult times and reach my goals.

There was always someone visiting my Grandparents' house—my uncle, aunt, cousins, Grandpa's cousin, who was also their financial advisor, or my mom's uncle. Of course, I was there most of the time, too, after kindergarten or school until I turned nine, and we moved to the western side of the town, to an area called Shahrake Gharb.

## *Kindergarten*

I started going to kindergarten. The kindergarten had a beautiful garden with Magnolia trees, and the kids used to run around them and play. But I was only there for a short time.

It was an old house on Mirdamad Boulevard, where the whole house had been turned into a kindergarten. Inside, the house was beautiful and bright, and the garden outside was green and decorative. I liked going there, and I liked the kids there, too. I never understood why they stopped sending me there.

## *Swimming Classes*

Mom registered me at the girls' swimming school close to our house the summer that I turned five. It was a beautiful pool in the garden of a big house. The pool was full of kids from 4 to 5 years old and older, who were divided into different groups.

Our group was taught in three-meter deep water because we knew how to keep afloat and move toward the edges with our feet paddling. The instructor would tell us to line up and jump into the water, holding our breath so the water wouldn't get into our lungs.

First, we learned frog-style, which, somehow, I wasn't fast at. Then we learned to crawl, which I loved, and I was quite fast, so much so that another girl and I were usually ahead of everyone else. I could hold my breath and breathe every three to five hand strokes, which made me quite a lot faster than the others.

During breaks, we would get a snack, and then we would get back into the pool to practice crawl and diving.

By the second year, when I was in the advanced group, I was elected to a competition. That was so exciting! They took us to a big pool called hijab for the area competition. Girls in Iran are required to wear a hijab by the age of 9. My mom was supposed to come, but she couldn't for some reason. I was so disappointed because all the other kids had their mothers with them.

On the day of the competition, I was a little intimidated. The pool was large and full of kids and adults waiting for their turn. There was a lady who announced names on a microphone. Our instructor was with us, and she talked to us to make us ready and inspired us to win.

When they called our names, we got ready. I tried to remember the tricks that make you move faster, how to do a fast dive start so that I didn't hit my stomach hard when entering the water, and how to push ahead. I knew I had to breathe at my full capacity so I could push forward and, at the same time, see a shadow of my fellow swimmers so I could guess if I was ahead or not. We had to do ninety-three meters, which was three rounds of the pool.

When I was close to the end of the first length, I turned and pushed as much as I could to use the power to get ahead. On the second length, I noticed one swimmer, out of four of us, had stopped, and the adults swam out to get her out. I wasn't sure why. The second round was about to finish, and I pushed with all my power to move forward.

Everyone was cheering for us, and I could see that I had gotten second place and won a silver medal. The distance between me and the other girl, who was ahead of me, wasn't that much—a three-second difference.

I was so happy and proud, but I felt lonely because my mother couldn't be there for something so important. Later, at home, they really cheered for me, though, and so did my grandparents, of course.

# CHAPTER 3

## Our Beautiful White House and My Family

### *My Oldest Memories*

At home, it was a different story from my grandparents' house. I had my Barbie dolls, their houses, and different toys to play with in my beautiful pink room. I was mostly anxious that my father might get angry with me and my brother for some reason and that the atmosphere would turn unpleasant. While he was a loving father, he was quite strict, like many other fathers around that time in my culture.

I couldn't understand the reason for his real anger back then. He had lost his parents in an air crash in the 1980s, and it was he who had bought the tickets for their trip. He blamed himself for their deaths, which I assume was one reason for his anger.

When I think about it now, I understand why there was tension all the time. It was because my mother was largely unsatisfied with my dad. He was not fulfilling when it came to her emotional needs. Romantically, they were close. She was also a middle child who was dependent on her parents, and this would make my dad angry at times. They were in their late twenties and maybe still not mature enough to handle the ups and downs of marriage themselves.

Our house was beautifully designed and always clean and tidy. My dad loved white, and they both had a sense of art. They had designed the house carefully.

My mom was a top student and had a bachelor's degree in law from the University of Tehran. She worked for the national oil company. Dad had also graduated from the University of Tehran, and he was an agronomist.

Dad used to work hard and was always busy in his office. He worked long hours and would leave early in the morning and come back at six or seven at night.

My mom worked for the first few years, and they put me in daycare from when I was 1 year old. I had a younger brother at the age of five, much to my parents' joy. However, I found it challenging to adjust to sharing the attention. Despite being the first grandchild and a particular favorite of my grandparents, I felt overshadowed by the new arrival. My mother's increased busyness added to my feelings of responsibility towards him, making life harder for me.

My grandparents used to watch me after kindergarten, and I would spend the rest of the afternoon at my grandparents' house until my mom picked me up after work.

Later, she quit her job when my brother was four years old to take care of us. For the rest of her life, she regretted that she had stopped working. She felt she had lost her independence. She had studied so much and was a top graduate. But after quitting her job, she didn't have a lot of friends or social interactions anymore and was kind of isolated as a stay-at-home mom.

## *My Father*

Dad worked hard back then. He and his partner owned a pesticide and fertilizer factory in the southwest of Tehran. Their office was a nice old house in the south part of the business area—Ferdowsi Square. It was a two-story house with big rooms and high ceilings. I always wondered who used to live there before the area became commercial, and Dad's company had bought it.

As a kid, I used to enjoy going to his office, where I would discover new things and play with office supplies. We would usually go during the weekend before we had our family lunch at a restaurant. I was always on the lookout to find something interesting in his office that he would give me permission to take home.

Those family times together were amazing for all of us. Still, I was always anxious that my behavior would be wrong or that Dad wouldn't agree with something that I said or did. I was never at peace.

It was different with my grandparents or when I was alone with my mom. Then I felt safe and relaxed, and I knew no one would lose it on me because I'd done something wrong. This feeling stayed with me as I grew up.

My father was born into a traditional, religious family that was proud of having old Tehrani roots. His father was an iron trader who owned a shop in the big Tehran Bazar. He was respected by many for his good manners and charm.

I never got to meet Dad's parents, as they died when I was one year old. We didn't talk about them much, either. I think it was upsetting for him to talk about the incident.

Every year, in February, we used to go to the graveyard where they were buried beside each other. Dad would clean up the site and put a bunch of fresh flowers on their graves, and he would pray for them. The way he looked, he was in deep thought. Then he would light up a cigarette as if he somehow needed something to deal with the pain. He would walk around, but he stayed completely silent.

The graveyard was located outside of Tehran in Beheshtzahra. Although I wasn't a big fan of the trip to Beheshtzahra, I felt it was my duty to respect my dad and show him that I would always be there for him. I knew it was a relief to him and that it helped to ease his pain somehow.

When we got there, my brother and I would take water to clean up the gravestones. Then, with my mom, we would pour some rosewater over the gravestones to clean them even more before putting flowers on the graves.

My dad was their eldest son. He used to tell us the story of how he'd asked his dad to support him financially so he could study for his postgraduate degree. He had gone to Sweden after he had studied at Uppsala University to study for his master's degree. He was highly appreciative that his father supported him and enabled him to study abroad because this helped him to become a successful businessman.

The story that I heard from my mom was that because Dad's parents had been arguing and had not been happy for some time, he had bought them tickets to go to Mashhad and visit the holy city of Iran, where one of the twelve imams is buried. People visit his shrine and pray there. This was around the time of the revolution.

On the way back, their plane crashed near Tehran because of miscommunication with the control tower. It was the beginning of a cold February, and everyone died as the plane crashed into the hills. It was a huge tragedy. I don't think Dad ever got over it.

I was five years old when he took me skiing for the first time. He put me in a ski school group class and sat down, reading a newspaper while enjoying the sunny, fresh mountain air. I was in the class the whole day and loved it.

Dad was scared of the road up to the mountain to the ski resort, so he would drive slowly and carefully. One of the times that he took me there, we were stopped and questioned by the committee, which is the law enforcement force that acts under the Ministry of Interior, at a stop check at the beginning of the road.

They asked him for his documents and then pointed at me. "Who is that?"

"My daughter," Dad answered, surprised by the question, and I guess caught off-guard because the next question was …

"Do you have your birth certificates?" We did not.

They let us go, but next time, we took our birth certificates with us.

I loved the mountains and snow and learned to ski pretty quickly. The ski trips with Dad were so much fun. He couldn't ski himself because he had broken his ankle skiing a few years before, and the doctors had recommended that he not ski again.

## My Mom

My mom was a kind human being. She was a smart, caring, passionate, and emotional woman, but she was not always happy.

My parents had a successful life financially, and it was largely her support that made Dad a successful man. They were loyal to each other, but I think she expected to have a better relationship, romance-wise. That made her feel sad and unsatisfied at times.

But my parents loved each other a great deal. Their relationship was like many other marriages, with good days and days of not understanding each other. Mom used to tell me, "It's important that, when a couple gets married, their families should be from the same background." I could understand that. Even though she always kept on good terms with my dad's family, she didn't have much in common with his sisters. I could tell that she wished she had the same family background, education, and social class. She shared this with me to make me understand how important it was.

In my young mind, I could see that one of my aunts, who was younger and closer to my mom, was committed to charity and religious events. My mom, being a spiritual person, always supported her. She would sometimes get involved just because it was something to do in honor of my late grandparents. She respected what my aunt did, but that was about it. They really couldn't connect in other ways.

My dad stopped talking to his older sister when I was eight years old, so I didn't see my cousins much. I didn't see my other aunt and uncle much, either, usually only during a New Year's visit. But, on my mom's side, I used to see my uncle and aunt at my grandparents' house and at family gatherings a lot. They lived close to my grandparents, too.

## *The Fall*

I started first grade at the beginning of the school year. I also cracked my forehead and went to the clinic.

My younger aunt, my mom's sister, wasn't married and was still living with my grandparents. She had an old cat that was always around. He was my playmate somehow, and I used to talk to him and invite him to my house in the garden. I was scared of his reactions, too, as he was big and would sometimes growl at me.

One day, while I was wearing Grandpa's slippers, which were too big for me, I was hanging around the porch and decided to run toward the kitchen. There was a dark, empty storage room next to the kitchen that

21

had a big freezer in it. My grandpa had recently returned from visiting his brother in Germany and had brought a lot of German chocolates with him. These chocolates were rare to find in Iran, which was experiencing a revolution and war. This was my definition of heaven. I was obsessed.

So, as I was running, I didn't realize that I had smashed the cat's tail with the big slippers, which caused him to yowl really loudly. When I turned back to the porch to check on him, he ran away up to the roof.

I ran through the house, past the kitchen, which led to the backyard, to make sure he was all right. But, in the kitchen, Grandma, who was cooking, had just mopped the floor, so it was quite slippery. Hence, I slipped and fell, hitting my forehead against the iron door that opened out into the backyard and the roof. I felt a little pain and numbness in my head as I fell.

The next second, my grandma was screaming, "Oh my God, why aren't you more careful? She's broken her head!"

They carried me back to the living room and put me down next to the gas heater. My mom arrived. She was really worried. I heard them saying, "Her head is broken. We should take her to the ER."

Mom took me to the clinic close to our house. A doctor and nurse took me inside and asked my mom to stay outside. The next thing I remember, the nurse was holding my hand, and the doctor was telling me, "Everything is going to be okay." There was green string and a giant needle above my head. I screamed with all my might … but I can't remember what happened after that. I guess the stitching was done.

When we headed back home, I saw my mom had been crying because her face was wet from her tears. I was surprised and asked her, "Were you crying?"

"No," she lied.

## Primary School Mirdamad

On the first day that Mom left me at school, I had mixed feelings. I was excited to meet the new kids and make new friends, but leaving my mom for this long caused a strange feeling. Anyhow, soon after she left, I got over it and began to enjoy the first day.

It was compulsory to wear a scarf and hijab at school. First graders had to wear a white scarf with their name sewn on the scarf so others would recognize them and be more caring and protective toward them.

But with my broken head, I had to skip the school uniform scarf and wear another type of scarf for a while. I had borrowed a little scarf from Grandma and wore it on top of my stitches.

The first few years of primary school were nice. I enjoyed learning how to read and write, and I soon found many friends to play with who invited me to playdates. The school staff was nice and friendly. They took care of us younger students well. However, there were a couple of incidents when they had to call my mom to school.

Once, I took Barbie dolls, a man and a woman, and their baby Barbie, to school to play with my friends during the break. Another time, I took a Sony Walkman that my dad had bought me to listen to music. The Walkman was thin, the size of a small pocket, and quite advanced for that time. I wanted to share it with my friends. However, these things were not allowed at school.

## *The Terror of the Bombs*

Iran had been at war with Iraq since 1981. I was in first grade when the bombing started. Although many years, maybe more than thirty-five, have passed since that time, I still feel the rush of anxiety when I hear a plane breaking the sound barrier and getting too close to the ground. There was an airshow last year that made me tense every time the planes got too close to the showground.

I remember the feeling of being afraid for our lives. My parents would rush to wake us up if we were sleeping. If not, we would run to stand under the doorframes to be safe.

The sound of the planes coming close, combined with the sound of the danger alarm going through town and the blackouts, was terrifying— fearing for our lives and not knowing if we would be alive the next second. Then there was the loud noise of a bomb hitting the ground and a big shake like an earthquake.

My mom would say, "They hit it!" and I was happy that it wasn't our house. Then, I would think of the poor people who had been killed and those who lay dying for days. The following day, their house and the rescue team would be in the news.

One time, our windows cracked because the house that they had bombed was so close to ours. I remember another time that they bombed a house just a few streets away from us.

Shelters had been created everywhere for people to hide when there was an air attack. In our school, they had opened the basement and made it into a shelter. When they took us down there, it was dark, damp, and scary. In my young mind, I imagined that if they hit the school and the building collapsed over our heads, I wouldn't be able to breathe. That scared me to death.

Another time, we were in my grandparents' house when the alarm went off just after the blackout had started. My mom rushed us under a doorframe. My grandparents were pale, and I felt an intense rush in my stomach. I didn't know what that feeling was. It was unknown to me as a child, but it happened every time there was an attack. Now I understand how anxious I was, thinking that we might die at any second.

The loud noise of planes getting closer to the ground, and then the bomb, Mom would say again, "They bombed!" It was a relief that it wasn't us that they hit. Yes, we were still alive! But what about those people who died? Who were they? Were there any kids? How could this even happen to them?

## Time with My Family

Until I was older, most days, my mom took us to my grandparents' house, and my aunt, uncles, and their sons would come, too. We all had lunch together. They joked a lot and laughed, sharing their experiences of the past few days. Whether something good or bad had happened to them, Grandpa or Grandma always gave them short but sincere and, most of the time, good advice.

After tea, we all knew it was time for Grandpa's afternoon nap. He would joke around and ask us to go away so he could go to his bed and pull his blackout curtains. I loved his bed. It was comfortable, and I loved its smell. It smelled like fresh linen, sometimes mixed with the cologne he would splash on his face after shaving every morning.

We would either leave when he went to bed, or we would stay and also have a nap. Mom, Grandma, and my aunt would chitchat, and I would rest in the other room until it was time to go back home.

We used to get coupons for sugar, sugar candy, rice, and other foodstuffs. One hot topic was that Grandpa had some coupons given to him as a veteran, and he wanted to share them with my mom, aunt, and uncle so they could get some basic food.

The news at the time was always about how many people had been killed. Pictures that showed the young soldiers who were heading to the frontline. The emotional songs they sang still give me chills when I hear them. You knew that many of those soldiers might never get back to their families, and, indeed, many got killed, captured, or were injured for life. The damage was beyond imagination.

Life wasn't easy, but it still went on. We still gathered late every afternoon at my grandparents' in spite of everything. We went to the swimming pool, sat on the swings with the cousins, and ate watermelon.

The second grade went by, and I learned how to read and write.

Dad drove me around in his blue Buick, and my mom seemed to be happier. My little brother was growing up and had turned three years old.

My grandparents' house was still my sanctuary. I loved it the most and spent most of my time there after school and during that summer.

# PART II

## Shahrak-e Gharb and My Education

# CHAPTER 4

## Moving to Shahrak-e Gharb

*Home with a View*

When I finished the third grade, we moved from the house across from my grandparents' to the western part of the city, farther away from them, to an area called Shahrak-e Gharb. We lived in a high-rise apartment block with a view.

Our condo was on the fourteenth floor. It was a beautiful apartment with a view of the city and airport on one side and the mountains on the other. When we moved in, it had a fresh paint smell, which was something I really enjoyed. And I loved the energy that the new, clean house had.

The best thing was that I made many friends in the playground. We played every day after school until the lights went out at eight p.m. That was amazing. Soon, I became close to a few girls who were running the show in the playground. We walked together all the time, talked to the boys, and played different games. The environment was completely different from where we had lived before.

There were four gated buildings in the complex, and they were all beautifully built. Most of them were occupied by young, well-educated families. We lived in the one called Nezami. The other three were called Khayam, Saadi, and Hafiz, all named after famous Iranian poets.

The playground and walking area in each building were beautifully made and maintained. People were nice and civilized, and the management of the buildings had implemented a lot of rules in order to keep everything disciplined. At the time, our building was managed by a retired army general. Kids, boys, and girls could talk and play freely without fear of getting arrested. This was important, even for me, a 9 year old.

We had my own customized childhood game, which we named Rabet. It was a variation of hopscotch, which captivated our hearts. The rectangular grid drawn out for the game used to be vast, offering ample space for two groups of kids to engage in friendly competition. Each team would strategically hop and jump across the squares, aiming to complete the course flawlessly while dodging the challenges and obstacles that lay ahead. It was the game that filled the air with our laughter. Back then, it wasn't just a game for us but a way of fostering bonds through the shared experience of Rabet.

We played Rabet as a group of kids, ranging from 9 years and upward, and it was so much fun. We played in the snow, on the grass with our bicycles, and in our homes.

One day, we pretended we had a pretend battle between our building and another building, Khayam. The boys were getting ready to fight, and the girls of Nezami were going to support them. I personally took this quite seriously. What felt right was that, for once, we were on the same level and in the same group as the boys. We had begun using the same facilities and playing in the same area. We also had the same rules, which was not the case outside of those gates.

In the girls' group, we would copy each other with things that we wore, like leggings or colored socks, and we would walk together in a group. Two of the girls, Sahar and Kathy were the trendsetters that the rest of us followed.

Sometimes, it was just the three of us walking together and talking to the other kids or to the boys. It felt more secure being in a group, and these two girls were confident doing so. My parents taught me to be self-conscious and always recognize right from wrong. I wanted to do the right thing, but even though I was confident inside, I was always analyzing my actions to make sure I was doing the right thing and that my actions wouldn't hurt anyone.

One thing that I didn't appreciate at the time was that when they made jokes about someone who was also there, the person was often not confident enough to defend herself. I guess that was a form of bullying, and maybe it had happened to me, too. I cannot remember, but to this day, I am sensitive to this kind of treatment and get furious if I see it being done to someone.

Those days, I wanted to defend those kids, too, but I wasn't able to. Instead, I had to stay calm and just watch. Today, I do my best to defend people if I see it happening, and I call it bullying, whether it involves children or adults, whether it's done by a president or a kid in the street. I just can't stand it.

There were a few kids that ruled, too! They were the leaders. I have remained friends with some of them until today, including the two brothers, Fardad and Farbod, who lived in the Hafiz building. The good memories of those days are irreplaceable.

There was a big, empty pool between our building and the Hafiz building. It had a dirty puddle of water mixed with mud and dirt and a beautiful big weeping tree. We used to run around the pool or jump from the big wall behind it. I think that wall was at least three meters high, and every time I jumped, I felt the pressure hitting the ground from that height. But the last thing in me was fear.

We would roll down a small grass hill or would meet in the playground, go to the small shop to buy gum, and, of course, by eight p.m., the lights were off, and I had to be upstairs.

A few times, one of the boys stopped me and asked for a kiss. All the other kids were there, too. I would get so shy and run away. I never let them kiss me.

Unfortunately, Iran and Iraq continued to be at war. The missile attacks on Tehran by the Iraqi government started the year after we moved to Shahrak-e Gharb. Therefore, we lived away from the city for almost nine months.

In those days, living in those buildings was so nice. They were happy days for kids, no matter what path they took in life. Those days are dear to me.

Later, when we moved to a bigger house on a street nearby called Iran Zamin, we still stayed friends and saw each other in school or would visit each other after school.

The bond I have with these friends is still strong. I believe that they feel the same way about me. We share this closeness because we lived in the same area as neighbors around the same time in our lives.

## A New School, Shahid Behzadi

The new school was nice and a lot bigger. I made many good friends and started the fourth grade there. My teacher, Ms. Asadi, was kind and caring.

The first few weeks went well. I liked my classmates. The schoolyard was spacious, and the fact that we were older was also nice. We liked to think we could rule the school.

Although there were still fifth graders who were more senior than us, I enjoyed going to school. I was focused and studied well. My results were always excellent. If I wasn't the first, I'd be the second highest in the class.

But those weren't happy days for Iran or Iraq. Many people were killed. The attack alarm went off constantly, and the blackouts and massive explosions from missiles that would hit a house or the ground are still hidden somewhere in my memory.

I was only years old. It was hard to fully understand the disaster that the country was going through and what impact it had on people, including my parents, who had us kids. I knew that my dad didn't have the tolerance to bear it, and he would rather leave Tehran and go somewhere where his family would be safe and sound, away from danger.

# CHAPTER 5

## Missile Attacks and Living in the North

### *Escape from the Missile Attacks*

This time, the missile attacks were harsher than before, with many innocent lives taken. Dad couldn't tolerate it. Even though the part of town we lived in was said to be safe, as soon as the attacks started, we packed our bags, got into our car, and headed north.

First, we went to join my aunt and my dad's sister. They were staying in a resort called Ziba Kenar, close to Anzali port in the northern part of Tehran.

For me, it was so much fun to hang out with other kids and my cousins all the time. I felt like we were always at a party, and I could play from morning until night. In one of the games, I learned from other kids how to catch frogs, tie a rope to their legs, and pretend they were racing together.

We stayed in a hotel in the same northern city for a couple of months. Then, we headed to the eastern side of the north part of Iran and stayed in the Hyatt Hotel. My brother and I found new friends.

The hotel was full of families, the same as ours, who were residents in a hotel now to get away from Tehran. We were all scared for our lives.

Mom and Dad also had friends there, happy hanging out with them. It was a small break from all the problems and bad news of war that was everywhere those days.

At that time, in that nice hotel, it felt like a new life, full of new people who saw each other all the time and had nothing else to do. It felt like a permanent holiday, but I was so young that I couldn't understand what my parents were going through. One thing I knew was they were worried about my education and studies, and they were searching for a school so that I could continue the fourth grade and not be held behind in my studies.

When we got settled, my parents decided to put me in the school in that town.

## From the School I didn't like to Freedom

We had breakfast, and then I left with Dad to go to the new school in the small city that used to be called Motelghoo but had changed its name to Motelghoo after the revolution.

I wasn't happy and didn't know what to do. I tried to talk to my dad about it a couple of times, but he stopped me and said, "It's best for you not to be away from your studies for such a long time." Education was a serious matter in our family. "You should learn your lessons at this school. Otherwise, it will be difficult for you to sit the fourth-grade exams."

"But I'm not used to a school like this," I told him. Even though I still wasn't sure, I just knew it would be different. However, I was scared to say anything else.

Dad stopped our red Renault 5 in front of the school doors, and I got out, reluctantly saying goodbye. I stepped into the school and started walking into the yard. It was a mixed school, and I felt that many of the kids were staring at me, making me uncomfortable.

Then, suddenly, a boy sarcastically said, "Oh, look, there's a Tehrani girl!"

I was so embarrassed and pissed off that I barely even looked at him before I turned around and walked out of the school.

My dad's car wasn't there anymore, so I returned to the hotel. It was about four miles away from the school. I was certain that I wouldn't return to a place I didn't like, so I crossed the main road parallel to the Caspian Sea, which goes along the coast, passing through various streets.

As I walked toward the hotel, I felt so free and happy. I was excited, too. I felt this feeling of freedom so deeply for the first time, and for the rest of my life, I have never forgotten it. It was the first time in my life that I tasted it, even though I was still a child.

Freedom is the basic right of any human. It shouldn't be taken away without any reason unless that person is harmful to society and other human beings.

I cherished freedom from that early age.

The sound of the big trucks and cars passing by was scary at first, but the fear quickly went away. Instead, my attention turned to a little butterfly that was on the ground, sitting without moving. I picked her up and noticed she had a broken wing, so I decided to take her with me and started chatting to her. I didn't even feel the impact of the distance that I had walked, as I was so busy enjoying nature and my little butterfly!

As I got closer to the hotel, I saw my dad's car had turned out of the exit toward the road. He stopped when he saw me.

In shock, my dad asked, "What on earth are you doing here?" I could see the disbelief and fear in his eyes.

"I left the school. I didn't like it, so I came back home," I replied simply.

He didn't say anything else as we went back to our room at the hotel.

My parents were concerned about the things that could have happened to me on the way. I was a nine-year-old girl, walking along the road that many cars had passed by. I could have easily been kidnapped, and many other things could have happened to me. At the same time, I could see the praise on their faces, as if they were secretly admiring my courage of walking alone for four miles … and walking away from what I didn't like.

Later, they told the story to my grandparents and a few friends. The only question that I was asked was, "Why didn't you like that school?"

"It wasn't nice," I told them.

## Village Villas and a Village School

From that hotel, we moved to a village villa. The villagers rented out their own houses to people like us, who had left their towns and cities because they were scared of the missile attacks in Tehran.

For me, it was quite nice, as all my family was there. I got to play with my cousins, and we were all together for a few months. We also visited some of my parent's friends who were staying at their villas close by. We barbequed and had a lot of fun, even though the war continued in our lives.

I started going to the village school. The classroom was small, and the boys had to be seated on one side and the girls on the other.

The kids were nice, and they were fascinated by the fact that I was a girl from Tehran. They wanted to make friends with me and talk all the time. The teacher was also quite nice and caring.

What wasn't nice was the physical punishment of students that I had never been faced with before. This, I found to be quite cruel.

If a student didn't do their homework and hadn't learned the lessons that they had been told to learn, the teacher would hit the palm of their hand with a long stick, hard, several times.

I made friends with a boy called Reza. We talked a little on the first day, and I asked him why he didn't have hair. He told me that they had shaved his head because of ticks.

I remember the day when my dad and his friend picked me up, and Reza waved at me and said with his northern accent, "See you tomorrow, Sarah." I saw Dad and his friend look at each other with wide eyes and smiles.

Then Dad asked, "Who was that guy?"

"He's my classmate. His name is Reza." And that was the end of that. I got in the car, and we drove away.

Reza hadn't studied well, so our teacher punished him with a stick. I felt so bad for him, but that was apparently normal. Then I asked why they punished kids physically. A bunch of other questions came to me, and I tried to figure out what it all meant.

I didn't understand what happened, but I only went to that school for a few days. I think my parents decided to just let the war pass until we could get back to Tehran, and I could get back to my own school. They may have come to the conclusion that going to school in another town in the north was too much of a change for a nine-year-old girl.

At night, we would have dinner with my grandparents, and my uncle and aunts would help clean up everything and get ready for bingo. It was fun. Grandpa read the numbers, and one of us kids was usually the winner.

After that, they would get together to play rummy while we kids played or did our own thing until we went to sleep.

I have colorful memories and happy thoughts from those times, in spite of the war and what was happening.

We visited Mr. Amini's, Dad's friend, villa a lot. He made us caviar fish kebabs, which were banned as they were not halal. But he had connections with the fishermen, and they brought him the freshest fish that he would barbecue on his fireplace in his beach villa for us. My brother and I played with the kids, and our parents hung out together.

There were other friends who we visited often in Shomal. One was General Shirani, who had served in the army with my grandpa. He had a villa close to the area where we were staying, and we used to visit him often with my grandparents.

The villa was not that big. It was a cute little cottage, and everyone used to sit and play cards. I was usually the only kid in the crowd when we went there, and because my grandparents normally took me there with them, I often sat with them. They would say I brought them luck, which I totally believed.

Sometimes, I would wait until they won and gave me some tips. But, most of the time, I'd go into the garden and explore. It was a massive garden that was mostly untouched. There was a narrow river on the side that divided the land with the house next to it. I used to pick up a stick and go watch the river. Sometimes, I'd see a water snake pass by or frogs and other creatures. I was scared of snakes, for sure. I think everyone, including their gardener, told me many times to be aware of the snakes in the garden. There were many around there.

One day, I was walking on the west side of the villa and saw something that looked like a little farm where they were cultivating something. I was in my own world, enjoying nature, with the smell of raw rice and green vegetables in the air.

Suddenly, a thick, pink snake swiftly passed between my feet. I jumped and started to scream, but no one was around. The snake didn't stop; it just continued to move. I was so shocked that I couldn't move for a few seconds, and then I ran screaming toward the villa and shared the story with everyone.

## *End of the War and Back to School*

The war that had started on September 22, 1980, a year after I was born, ended after a lot of bloodshed, with many lives taken and homes destroyed on August 20, 1988.

So many innocent people had been killed, and so much damage had been left behind. The long-term mental health issues that it caused to people of both countries still continue to surface to this day.

Everybody was so happy, even though the effects of it still stayed for a long time. I remember the relief and tremendous happiness that was in the air.

That was when I started fifth grade with some of my previous peers. We were all top students but had a lot of fun in the classroom, too.

That summer, after the war had ended, it was like the country had gotten a new life. You could see the smiles on everybody's faces. People were happy that, after eight years, life was getting back to its normal routine. There was no more fear of air attacks or young people being killed on the frontline.

In fifth grade, we used to pick at the way our teacher, who was kind and caring, pronounced a word. My friend Sahar, who used to sit next to me, and I would look into each other's eyes and laugh. Sometimes, it would get out of control, and we would have to go under our desks.

I shared this with my dad and how it might get me into trouble, and he suggested I pretend to have toothache if it happened again, and we couldn't stop laughing.

As soon as Mrs. Darbandi said a word with a funny accent, and we were about to crack up, I would put my finger on my tooth and pretend my tooth was aching. It really did help me stop laughing. It was a simple distraction.

That year ended well and with many nice events and happy memories. I did well in my studies, and all my grades were good. This made my parents, especially my mom, proud, and she talked about it with my grandparents.

We decorated our classroom in February, which was the anniversary of the Islamic-Iran revolution. My birthday was at the beginning of the ten days when they would celebrate the so-called Daheie Fajr, which means "ten days of victory."

There were all sorts of celebrations that we would prepare for, too, in those ten days. Preparing to sing revolutionary songs and theater performances were some of them.

## *Grandpa's New Villa*

Grandpa decided to build a villa on land that he owned around the same town in the north where we had stayed before during the missle attack. Everyone was excited as he got busy with his plan.

The villa was soon built, and all the family went there and stayed for holidays. Those trips were the best that I have ever had in my entire life. Having so much love around me, with my parents, grandparents, uncle, and aunts, was amazing.

We played, went to the beach, ate BBQ corn that they sold at the beach, and rented ponies to ride on. We cooked delicious food and ate together. We played cards or bingo and went for long walks in the jungle together. How amazing it was to be around my family and how lucky I was to have such a loving family.

With cousins who were all boys, we were always exploring and discovering in the garden or outside of the villa. We were not allowed to go too far, but we barely stayed inside. We always ran around and played, and talked to the people from the village, some of whom were local farmers.

We visited the town center often, where grownups wanted to buy handicrafts, jams, fresh food, and fruit, and we were given some money to buy a little candy or chocolate, too. We went to the beach to swim in the mornings.

Of course, there were separate areas covered with tents for men and women. They were far from each other, as men and women were not allowed to go to the beach together. So, I went to the designated area for women with my aunt, mom, grandma, and my uncle's wife. There were always people who were there to ensure that nobody got out of the tent area with a bikini or without a proper hijab.

It was still nice to go to the Caspian Sea and swim. My biggest goal was to find nicely shaped stones for my stone collection, which I was proud of. I loved that I always found really nice, beautiful colored stones.

One of the stones that I found while praying to God and asking Him questions later in life I have kept to this day. The meaning is so deep to me because it looked like it had the shape of God engraved on it.

The north of Iran carries the most beautiful memories for me, especially about my childhood.

# CHAPTER 6

## Middle School and Friends

### *6th Street, Iranzamin*

We moved to another house in the same area, on Iranzamin Street, and I started middle school. I made friends with our neighbors, who had two daughters, Bahar and Sara.

We had snowball fights in the winter and went to the pool in the summer. We rode bicycles and enjoyed being outdoors.

One of our neighbors also had three kids, and another had two kids. Most afternoons, we used to go into the little garden, put our mats on the ground, and make flowers or food with playdough. We would pretend we had a shop and go to each other's houses and buy "groceries" from each other. It was really fun.

It was around the time of the FIFA games in 1990 when Roth Goliath was famous, and there were pictures of these soccer players sold with chewing gum called Fifa. We used to buy the gum and collect the pictures.

My collection and our neighbor's son's, Sam, collection were quite good. They were some of the best soccer players, and we used to exchange pictures. It was important for us, as kids, to have a big collection at the time, and we kept showing off our pictures to each other.

Every morning, I would wake up and make myself ready to get to the front of the street and wait for the bus. I'd usually meet Sara, who went to the same school as me for a couple of years, and we laughed and talked.

I often misjudged the weather. I wouldn't think that it might be cold in the morning and go out without enough layers. Therefore, I would get cold waiting for the bus.

All the houses on those streets were beautiful and nice. The house in front of ours had been given to people who had lost their homes in the border cities during the war. It didn't have windows, and they had covered them with carton papers and blocks, which made the house look ugly from the outside, even though it was a nice, white building. I used to wonder what happened to them, how their lives were now, and what would happen to them in the future.

Apart from snowball fights with other girls in the neighborhood, we would also take our bicycles and ride in the streets. We had birthday parties, and life was really good.

My parents wanted me to learn to play the piano, so they bought one and got a teacher for me and my brother. Mr. Ata played amazingly himself, and he tried hard to teach me the notes, but his tuition didn't have much of a result because I barely paid attention. Finally, he put numbers on my fingers that helped me read the notes and play the songs. So, I learned to play that way and memorized a few of my parents' favorite Iranian and classic songs that made them happy. But that was it. One of Dad's favorites was called "Lime Light."

Dad used to play without notes and sing in the mornings, which made all of us laugh. He wouldn't stop and would sometimes play for half an hour. Eventually, we had to beg him to stop, as he would play songs that he would make up without notes or rhyme.

My youngest brother was born when I was thirteen, and he made us all even happier. I was a little hesitant at first about whether I was happy about it or not. I thought it might be too late for my mom to have another child. When he was born, however, I loved him so much. He was the cutest little boy, who was always smiling. I was so protective of him.

Mom and Dad, and even my grandparents, became busy when my little brother was born. I was busy with my smart friends, too, mostly studying and reading the encyclopedia.

The students were ranked from the top, and I always competed between second and third.

I think it was around the same time that the TV satellite dishes came to Iran, and people had them installed in their houses so they could see foreign channels and movies. One of the channels was called Star TV. I remember their logo was a star, and the song was well-known.

I was growing up fast. I had brought a street cat from our neighbor's house on the street behind our house. He was a little kitten and super cute. We took him to the vet. Even though my mom didn't like cats much, she let me keep him. My room was on the other side of the house, and I let the cat sleep in my bathroom.

One night, we all woke up to find that the house was shaking. It was an earthquake! Mom and Dad took us outside quickly. Everything was shaking really hard. It was so scary. Everyone else was also in the street. After a minute or so, it stopped, and everybody, although still scared, went back inside.

I remember that the degree certificates from the University of Tehran, which my parents had framed and were so proud of, had fallen off the wall and broke.

The next day, we saw on TV that the epicenter of the earthquake was in a northern town in the mountains called Roodbar, and the strength was 6.8 on the Richter scale. So many people were killed in that earthquake. It was a national disaster. Unfortunately, even though Tehran was known to be a town that was prone to earthquakes, the majority of houses back then were not earthquake-proof, and, of course, the villages and other cities were the same, so they were completely destroyed.

## Ski with Modern Sport

Dad signed me up for a ski school tour called Modern Sport. They used to come and pick me up around three or four a.m., and we had such an amazing time on the bus getting to the mountains, skiing all day, and then heading back to Tehran. Of course, there were days when I was not allowed to go. Whether it was because I had to study more or because there was another reason, I don't remember, but it would make me so sad. I would even wake up when I heard the minibus come onto our street to pick me up, but I wasn't there. I was hoping a miracle happened and Dad would let me go. Then, I would fall back to sleep.

Skiing was like going to heaven, even though, while the minibus was moving through the mountains, the movement mixed with the smell of gasoline would always make me dizzy. But we would pick up all the ski students from our neighborhood, whom I had made friends with, although most of them were older than me. And being in the same place with all the other kids all the way to the resort, without any grownups, parents, or teachers, was something completely new.

The whole drive to get to the mountain was around an hour, and then we'd ski all day until we got back around 4 p.m. It was really fun.

Modern Sport would take us to one of the ski resorts called Shemshak. There were security stops on the way where the committee would check on us. The bus driver would turn the music down, and they would sometimes come up to the minibus and check if the girls had too much makeup on. Usually, it was a short stop, and we would be let go.

For me, it was still stressful. When we were stopped for a security check, I was always anxious that we wouldn't be able to get to the resort or that something would go wrong.

When we got to the resort, the fresh, crisp smell of the air was amazing and so refreshing. I still appreciate my parents' courage in allowing me to experience this in my youth.

We used to put on our ski shoes, buy tickets, and then get to the cabin lines. Back then, girls and boys had separate ski areas, and we had to make sure our hijab was complete. We also had to wear a long tunic, called a "badgir", that covered us up to the knees. They checked that the girls were properly dressed on their way to the resort, but we still had a great time with all those restrictions.

There was a restaurant in the middle of the resort where everybody stopped and hung out. We somehow got to talk to the boys freely, even though we were still controlled by the committee. There was less pressure, and we got to stand in the same line and use the same cabin to go up the mountain. We also sat together in the same restaurant without fear of being arrested.

This was a huge deal for a young girl who was afraid of everything relating to school and society, who didn't want to disappoint her parents in any way, especially by getting arrested for doing something wrong, like talking to a boy! But, in the resort, it was like the pressure was less, and the local people or committees who were supposed to control these things were also not as strict.

It couldn't be better than to be able to ski all day, meet friends, and hang out semi-freely with the girls and boys you knew. There was no alcohol or partying allowed, but this was still priceless for teenagers like me back then.

I enjoyed the crisp mountain air, snow, and sunshine so much, especially since I had been skiing from when I was five years old when my dad used to take me there.

I became a good skier, and ski days became the most important days of my life. There was always a competition to see who could ski around the most. I lived for winter and the ski season.

## 2nd Street, Iranzamin

I was officially a teenager.

We moved a couple of streets down from where we used to live right before my little brother was born, and we lived there until I left Iran. I asked for my room to be painted navy blue—everywhere, even the ceiling.

We lived in a beautiful two-level house on the street opposite a big mall that had recently been opened. It was called Golestan, where we'd go a lot as teenagers, and it was where other kids gathered and socialized.

We had a little pool and yard where my dad often gardened. My room, my parents' living room, the guest room, and the kitchen were upstairs, and my brothers' rooms and Dad's office were downstairs.

They designed the house beautifully, and Mom was happy that she could pick her favorite furniture and paintings for the living room. She used to do vitray painting (painting on glass) before she had gotten married to Dad. At my grandparents' house, all the glasses on top of the doors were her artwork.

The house was located on a dead-end street, which was connected to the end of the next street by a park. It was beautiful and green.

Our neighbors were nice, too, and I got close to our neighbor's daughter, who was the same age as me. Nousha and I hung out once in a while at their place or ours. Her room was a loft and had a window that opened onto the roof. We used to go there and sit and talk about our dreams and wishes, which, as teenagers, included a long list.

She was beautiful, she used to wear a lot of mascara and spend a lot time doing make up. I didn't have the patience to do so much makeup. I also found myself kind of scary-looking when I wore too much makeup!

In the second year of middle school, I met a friend who was big on sports. She was tall and athletic, and she played basketball and was an amazing horse rider. I also got interested in basketball, and we soon became close. Golnaz has remained one of my dearest friends to this day.

My other friends were Donia, Asal, and Arezou. They were always my competition in school because of their top grades—usually twenty out of twenty. I sat next to them in class and was the third-to-top student in the class after them, always with a mark of eighteen or nineteen out of twenty which was the school scoring system in Iran.

We would read the encyclopedia for fun and learn about cities and countries, movies, actors, books, and science. We would also play a game before class started in the morning or during break. Our game was a word puzzle. We had two teams. They would tell us how many letters were in a word that they had chosen, and then we had to guess letter-by-letter what the word was. That was a fun game, and I learned a lot of general knowledge.

One of our friends had a long-term boyfriend, and they had kissed. It was so interesting to hear about the way they kissed and how it felt. We sat with her and listened carefully. It seemed like she was ahead of us in experiencing this.

Our school building and the grounds were quite big. We had a basketball net and a volleyball net in the front, as well as a nice café and a little yard in the back. The teachers and the dean were friendly. I never felt any discomfort as long as I followed the rules.

The friends I used to play with at our first house were also in the same school, and we always studied, played, and shared our experiences that we had with boys. My mom would pick me up after school and ask if I wanted to go anywhere with her. If I had another class, I'd go home and get prepared for my classes, such as English, art, etc. Otherwise, we'd go to my grandparents' house.

My grandparents eventually came to the conclusion that their house was too big for them to manage anymore. This was after they had been burglarized while they were sleeping. They were shocked and scared.

Therefore, they moved into a condo in the same neighborhood in the upper center of Tehran called Mirdamad.

Going to their house always put a smile on my face, even just ringing the bell and hearing my grandpa say, "Sarah!" with a joking voice, as if he was surprised that I was there, though I knew he'd been expecting us.

Entering their second-floor condo, I knew I would be pampered for the rest of the time I was there. I could say whatever I wanted, and everyone still adored me. Grandma would praise me with her loving words, and Grandpa would constantly joke around, trying to make me laugh.

I know I was such a spoiled girl, but it was this love that fulfilled my future. And it still burns inside me, even many years after that they have been gone, resting in heaven. The love in the air in their house was so tangible that I could still feel it in my heart years after they had passed.

## Soap

It was around this time that I started to get an obsession with soap. It started with one particular soap that Grandpa used to buy from the community market near their house. Every time I washed my hands with it, I smelled it deeply. The smell was so amazing that I couldn't stop. I was obsessed to the point that I took one from Grandpa, brought it home, and started grinding it. While I was doing that, I could smell it more, and this had a relaxing sensation for me.

I kept breathing deeply so that I could smell its intensity. Of course, I wasn't snorting it, but it made me cough badly. Regardless, I kept grinding the soap to make a floury powder. Then, I would add water to it and shape it into different things. Gradually, I bought different types of soap and asked my grandpa to give me one once in a while. The big wardrobe in my room became full of soap and the things that I had made out of it. I really enjoyed this process.

My parents were worried that it affected my lungs. Anyone who went into my room could smell the soap. One of my cousins once pulled out my desk drawer without realizing that the powder was in there. It shook the powder into the air ... and into his nose. He coughed for half an hour, and tears were running down his face, which made us laugh a lot.

At night, when I sat together with Mom, Dad, and my brothers, I kept grinding and chopping soap. It would give me a peaceful feeling inside.

I'm not sure what caused this obsession. Later, it changed to making candles of different shapes, using milk pockets and ice. I added them to my soap collection and held an exhibition. I made a few grand selling my soap and candles.

The obsession lasted until I went to university. Gradually, it faded, but I still keep soap and essential oils in my drawers. The smell takes me into a garden full of flowers and lavender, and it resets my brain.

## Skiing with Golnaz

By this time in highschool, Golnaz was my best friend. She was a really good skier and a member of the national ski instructors' team. Her parents had an apartment close to Dizin Ski Resort in a village called Gajere, and they stayed there during the season or for the Iranian New Year.

Golnaz invited me to go with her during the Iranian New Year holiday. Her parents and their group of friends were all going, and they all had kids who would hang out at the resort and ski all day.

It was important to us how many rounds we got going up and skiing down the slopes. Golnaz was athletic and also competitive. But, as much as I enjoyed skiing and the mountains, I also enjoyed relaxing and being in the sun.

The first day that we went skiing, I forgot to put any sunblock, and my face got so badly burnt that it was painful, and my skin started to peel. It was not a good experience. I had never burnt my facial skin so badly. It was a lesson that taught me to always try to protect my face after that.

Later on, I was proud to be able to tell people how much I used to ski. And they could see from my suntan that I had been out on the slopes! But I didn't follow them up and down the slopes all the time. My ski style was good but not as good as Golnaz's. I didn't find much joy in skiing too fast, either.

I spent my days skiing, slower than them, and stopping at the middle restaurant to have some tea and sunbathe, talking to friends who also stopped by.

All in all, that was a fun trip.

# CHAPTER 7

## High School and Changes

### *February 1st*

February 1st is my birthday.

On this date, 45 years ago, Imam Khomeini returned to Tehran after spending four years in exile in Paris. His arrival followed the success of the Islamic Revolution, which overthrew the Kingdom of Iran. Since then, the country has been known as the Islamic Republic of Iran.

I want to share the experiences my compatriots and I had, particularly the challenges faced by women in Iran. It is important to acknowledge the changes that have occurred over time. Additionally, having spent more than two decades in the Western world, I have come to realize that there is a lack of awareness among many about the life, culture, and society in Iran, particularly in light of the developments of the past four decades.

### *The Strict School*

Our high school was more like a prison than a school, or it felt that way to me. The walls were more than three meters high. The basketball court and volleyball grounds were separated by a few stairs. The toilets were cleaned every day, but they were still usually dirty and stank badly. The school building had more than two floors, with a teacher's office and dean's office at the front and classrooms at the back.

To me, going to school every day was like going to prison, spending five hours with slaving monsters. I don't know if it was the same for the others, but that was how I felt. As soon as we stepped onto the school grounds, I was under pressure to be a good student, not only to study properly but mainly to maintain principles and follow the school's strict rules.

The rules that were controlled by principles included the Islamic hijab, no makeup, no hair showing out of the veil, and no plucked eyebrows or dyed hair. If someone got their eyebrows done and dyed their hair, they had to attend evening school and weren't allowed to attend morning school like ours anymore.

Also, our behavior in and out of school was always controlled. If we were caught talking to a boy out of school after school hours, the next day, we were called and questioned and possibly expelled.

Our dean, Mrs. Rezai, was the scariest of all. She was a tall, big-boned woman with a lot of hair on her upper lip and eyebrows, showing that she hadn't removed any of it for a long time.


## Pain

Around the same time, I started getting my monthly cycles, and I became sick during that time. The pain made me throw up, my head would get cold, and my blood pressure was really low. When that happened, I had to head to the office and ask them to call my mother.

A couple of times, I ended up in Mrs. Rezai's arms. I don't know how, but I saw her face close up! Other times, they took me to the prayer room, which was covered in carpets, where the students gathered to say Friday prayers together. Sometimes, the principals would ask the students to go there to pray. The rest of the time, whoever wanted to go there for prayer could.

The pain was always unbearable. My mom would fetch me and take me to the nearest hospital or clinic, where they would inject me with Diclofenac, an anti-inflammatory and strong pain medication. I couldn't breathe from the pain. It's hard to describe, but I just kept turning around to try to cope with it. Then, as soon as the painkiller was injected, in a few seconds, the pain would start to lessen, and I would become calmer and more relaxed.

Sometimes, before we got to a clinic, my mom would warm my stomach with a hot towel and massage it, which would help. The rest of the time, however, we had to get to a clinic. I couldn't even cry, but I kept asking God for the pain to stop, as it was unbearable.

They tried injecting Hyoscine, which was an antispasmodic drug, and a few other painkillers, but the most effective one was Diclofenac, which was also the most dangerous because one side effect was paralysis. I still got the pain later on in life, but I learned how to manage it.

During those years, it was severe, and I often wondered if it was related to the stress of the situation that caused a physical reaction. It was as if, as a teenager, I had to deal with so much emotional trauma that it turned up as terrible pain in my body every month.

## *No Freedom*

Every morning at school, we had a morning program where we had to stand in long lines and keep our distance from the person in front of us, holding up a straight hand in line with the next person's shoulder to measure the distance. First, one of the students read some of the Quran. Then, we had to say a few sentences that we repeated every morning. One student would read, and all the others would repeat after her. There were about two hundred students.

The morning slogan was: No Western, no Eastern, Islamic Republic. Independence, freedom, Islamic republic!

Freedom was a concept that I could barely feel or understand in those days when everything, everywhere, felt so suffocating. I couldn't see why this word was part of our slogan and why we had to repeat it every morning.

Did everyone else feel like me, or was it just me and my personal issues? I still cannot tell. But what I could see was that my friends and fellow students who were in the same school sometimes had the worst family problems. This made freedom a remote possibility.

I was lucky that I was born into a family with parents who were educated. My parents were proud that they were graduates of the country's best university. And I was lucky to have parents raising me who had the knowledge and open views about good and bad. Neither of them was interested in politics.

I remember my dad admiring how charismatic Imam Khomeini was. I guess they wanted me to recognize right and goodness more than anything else and to stay away from trouble. It wasn't the same with all families.

A representative and school supervisors would walk between the lines while we were busy listening to the morning program, checking our uniforms, making sure that our faces and nails were clean, and that we weren't wearing makeup. If you weren't neat and clean, you were in trouble and would be dragged out and sent to the principal's office to explain why. They would deduct marks if you appeared to have a lack of principles.

If there were major problems—for instance, if they caught you with a boy outside of the school or something similar—you were expelled straight away.

Growing up in Iran after the revolution, I was never able to witness the country's pre-revolution era firsthand. Whenever my grandparents shared their nostalgic recollections of a bygone time when Iran's lifestyle was often compared to the lifestyle in the West, I longed for a glimpse of that world. My grandparents' stories would often make me crave to experience what Iran looked like back then. It was evident from their tales that back then the country had a very different environment, with a mix of both tradition and modernity. Unfortunately, the suppression system in the country during my childhood and teen years made it impossible for me to experience something like that in my life. It made me crave more for freedom.

## First Grade of High School

In highschool there were girls who were eighteen years old in the last grade, were now completely grown up. I was still young, probably one of the youngest, as I had started school a year early.

Since the staff was much stricter than the middle school, I definitely felt a little rebellious, not liking the pressure.

The teachers weren't as friendly as before. Whether it was the students who made them frustrated or the amount of material that they had to teach distracted students, I don't know. Or maybe, somehow, it was just the culture of that school.

At the beginning of the school year, the principal, Ms. Parsi, asked me to become the classroom ambassador. I refused her offer as I was pulling toward anything that distracted me from the pain of that environment, let alone being an ambassador. From then on, the principal turned her back on me, always watching me to catch me doing something wrong.

I was shy when it came to getting to know other students, though I already knew some from middle school.

Golnaz and I were in the same class. We sat at the same desk, and I studied hard to keep up with the high school modules that were a lot more demanding than those in middle school. I had chosen science, so I had to read a lot and remember physics, chemistry, Arabic, and math. New mathematics was something totally new to me, and I hated it. The new math teacher, Ms. Sattari, had a strong northern accent and was quite strict and harsh toward us students. She was impatient and unkind, shouting for no reason, and always made me nervous.

It was at this time that, instead of listening to her, we were busy carving into our wooden desks with the first letter of the boys we fancied. I had carved a big M, Golnaz an H, and Donia a K. It was our way of entertaining ourselves during the most boring of classes.

One day, at the beginning of class, a school administrator knocked at the door and called me to go for a news interview in the school. I was so happy to be able to get away, but when I got back to class, Ms. Sattari called me to her desk.

"What is the carved M on your desk all about?" she asked. "I don't know and didn't do it," I claimed, surprised and scared.

"I've done it all myself. Now you want to trick me?" she replied sarcastically, but she didn't continue with her anger, as she had a smile on her face.

I went back to my desk.

"She saw the carvings on the desks when you were away.

She asked us about them, too," Golnaz whispered to me. We were scared, but the whole class was smiling.

At the end of the year, I passed that course, but with the lowest mark.

We played basketball during the break unless was at lunchtime and we wanted something to eat. Since Golnaz was tall and good at the game, she mostly played with final-grade students, who were also pros. At the same time, I was learning the moves and shoots.

After school, we usually walked home, which was within two miles of the school.

The boys used to cruise around the school in their cars. Our dean would also drive around, making sure students, who were all female, weren't talking to boys or getting into one of their cars.

We were afraid to see Mrs. Rezai's big, old white Mercedes Benz coming from afar, even if we weren't doing anything wrong. We were afraid she would find something wrong with our behavior that would cause trouble at school.

One day, while we were playing basketball, Golnaz heard us being called to the office on the intercom. We quickly ran into the school office, fearful of what was wrong.

One of the principals, Mrs. Farahi, told Golnaz, "Your scarf is so worn; you need to change it. The black is fading. You both need to wear your hijab better. And Golnaz, you need to wear longer pants." Golnaz seemed to be getting taller.

We smiled and said yes with a giggle, but we were scared and rushed out of the office.

We couldn't stop laughing, especially because of what she had said to Golnaz. We found it funny, it felt as if we had won a kind of victory. They couldn't find anything wrong other than our uniforms!

I joined the school's basketball team and got time out to go to basketball matches outside of the school against other school teams. I remained on the bench most of the time as a reserve, but Golnaz became the school basketball captain. Our team won the regional games, and we went to competitions at a basketball stadium a few times. This was a great getaway.

## Second Grade of High School

In the second grade of high school, Golnaz and I were in the same class again and soon became friends with three more students: Yasaman, Setareh, and Rana. We sat at the last three desks in the right corner, next to the windows. Another student, called Tina, sat next to me. Yasaman and Setareh were behind me, and behind them sat Rana and Golnaz.

I also again met Maryam, my primary school friend, but she was in the next-door class. We started talking during breaks, and a big part of our talk included boys. I still didn't have a boyfriend, but I was fascinated by the idea of meeting someone and falling in love.

We had a lot of laughs in the classroom about different teachers, imitating how they taught. Being a group of five girls gave us confidence, and we have stayed friends to this day. But I couldn't care less about studying.

Maryam, her parents, and her older sister, Ana, lived a few minutes away from us. Maryam's mom was our physics teacher. She had also taught our class in the third grade. She was serious but kind at the same time. My mom spoke to her, and I started going to their house for extra physics classes after school.

Other teachers came to our house, or I'd go to their houses so they could help me with math, chemistry, and other subjects. After all, not being a good student was unacceptable in our family, especially to my mom.

Of course, I studied less and less at school. Everything had become like a silly joke to me. I was becoming a complete rebel.

## *Khane Darya, Northern Holiday Resort*

Golnaz's family had a villa in the north of Iran, Shomal, which is a resort by the sea called Khane Darya. They used to go there in March during the Persian New Year holiday or at the end of summer in September. My best memories go back to the times when I was invited to go with them. Sometimes, Yasaman would come with us, too.

Although her mom had many rules we had to follow, we would have so much fun during those holidays. Rules of the house made by Auntie Sherry included washing the dishes after breakfast, lunch, and dinner and cleaning the house before we were allowed to go out. We had a midnight curfew so we wouldn't get home too late.

We would follow the rules closely to make Auntie Shirin and Uncle

Sam happy and make sure that nothing would affect the time that we could spend out.

After breakfast, we would leave the house to go to the beach. We would go to the café where everyone used to gather under a wooden dome located at the beach. We would sit there and meet up with some other teenagers or go for a ride in Golnaz's dad's car all around the gated community. She didn't have a driver's license, but she was tall and drove her dad's black Nissan Patrol. We called the car Khosro, which is a man's name. I don't know why we had a name for the car.

We listened to Alabina or Gipsy Kings a lot as we drove around, although we couldn't leave the resort since Golnaz didn't have a license. But it was a big resort, and there were enough places to go.

The villa next door to them belonged to her aunt. Her cousin, Nima, was also there, and he sometimes took us around in his car or just hung out with us.

We would go back to the villa just before lunch to help set the table and get ready to eat at noon with Uncle Sam and Auntie Shirin. When we had eaten our lunch, we would go to the room and talk. We had so much to talk about and analyze, whether we fancied or were dating a boy, or what had happened that day, or the plans we had for that night. We were always excited and couldn't wait to get out again. From six to seven p.m., we would leave the house again to meet up with friends or go to the café at the beach.

At night, it used to get crowded. Of course, the committee controlled everyone and ensured that teenagers like us followed the rules and didn't do anything dangerous.

All the people we knew would gather there, and it was like a big party every night. This did not include drinking or smoking openly. Sometimes, we would get a hot dog or pizza.

There was a track next to where a road was going to be built. It ran alongside the sea, then turned back toward the beachfront. We called it the three-kilometer road. We would play loud music and drive there fast. It was so freeing, so exciting, and we were so happy to be able to drive fast over the wide bumps in the road constructed to slow cars down. We knew we were in a safe place where teenagers and older youngsters could meet and socialize.

Although there were still a lot of regulations, there were fewer than back in Tehran, and we had relatively more freedom. In Khane Daarya, we knew lots of people from different parts of town, mostly the same kids who would go skiing, as well, and they all knew each other.

Nima, Golnaz's cousin, was mostly with us. We knew his friends and would talk to them and laugh a lot at the beach.

There were two places where we used to gather with others—a pizza restaurant in the middle of the gated resort and a beach restaurant.

Yasaman my other classmate, came with us on one of the best trips we ever had. We didn't stop laughing the whole trip. One thing we laughed at a lot was the way Yasaman woke up in the morning. She yawned and made loud groaning noises, but she wouldn't respond when we asked her if she was awake. This went on for forty minutes until we finally started "attacking" her with pillows to wake her up.

One day, while Yasaman was cleaning the dishes, I went to clean the toilet. Our towels were all the same color, and when I brought them back from the toilet, they got all mixed up in the kitchen, and Yasaman was using them to dry the breakfast dishes.

We realized the disaster and were cracking up laughing while we shared what had happened with Golnaz. Just as we were about to rush outside, Golnaz said, "Shut up and don't say anything. Let's just finish up and get out."

We laughed about that for many years. It still makes us laugh thinking about Golnaz's mom's reaction if she knew what had happened.


## *Getting Stoned*

That trip was amazing. It was also one of the first times that I smoked marijuana.

That night, Golnaz was with some of her other friends at the beach. Yasaman and I were with Nima and his friends. We went to a quiet, nonresidential side of the resort to smoke weed. We hung out together and, being quite stoned, laughed a lot. Then we went to the beach to find Golnaz so we could get back to the villa together before our midnight curfew.

Golnaz and her boyfriend had already ordered pizza and hot dogs, and they had ordered extra for us, too. We ate them all, then got back to the villa, still stoned.

"Are you still hungry? I am," I asked Yasaman. She giggled. "Yes, very."

We were hesitant to ask Golnaz because we wouldn't dare open the fridge. But, while she was in the bathroom, brushing her teeth, I went to the fridge secretly and opened the door, where I found a tray of baklava and took it back to the room. Yasaman also took some, and then I quickly took it back in the fridge.

Of course, Shadi Joon, being aware of everything in the house, found out, and a few minutes later, Golnaz came to the room, so surprised, and said, "Are you guys still hungry?"

We didn't want her to know that we had smoked weed and that it had made us more hungry, so we replied, "No," together, trying to hide what we had done.

"How can you still be hungry after all the pizza and hot dogs we ate at the beach?"

At that point, we couldn't stop ourselves from laughing and told her that we had smoked with Nima her cousin. That was why we were so hungry!

## Back in School

One day, Golnaz pulled her scarf over her face to cover her chin. She put on glasses and started to imitate our physics teacher on the blackboard. Her back was toward the door, so she didn't see that the teacher had arrived. She was standing there for a few minutes, watching her talk in a weird voice, as if she was teaching physics.

We were all laughing loud on the floor when she finally turned around, saw her, and got back to her desk. The more serious the teacher got, the more jokes we made and the more rebellious we were.

Another time, we had a physics exam, and none of us studied. We didn't even understand much of what she had taught in her lessons because we barely paid attention. We were just wasting time, trying to do something to make the time pass more quickly.

I was sitting in the third row from the end, and there was a heater between me and the wall. I realized that I could cheat by copying Tina, a girl who sat next to me. She was a good student who got good marks. So, I passed my paper to Maryam and Yasaman at the back, and they passed it to Golnaz and Rana, who were sitting behind them, so that at least we could all write something.

During the next physics class, the teacher called my name. She also called Golnaz and asked us both to stand up. "How are both your answers exactly the same? Explain to me, please. How can that be possible while you are sitting two benches apart?"

We had smiles on our faces and didn't feel ashamed. Somehow, we felt victorious about our magnificent way of cheating and answered, "We don't know. That is not possible." Of course, we all got low marks, and I had to retake that course again in the summer.

It was great entertainment to have in that school where almost everything was restricted. It was like another getaway. The café had halal ham sandwiches that everyone would fight over to buy during the break. Golnaz, being a tall girl, could usually reach to buy some, so we would give her our money. If the halal ham didn't taste good or looked soggy and limp, we would usually buy a packet of Cheetos that was called pofak in Iran, replace the ham with that, and eat it with pickles and tomato. It was so yummy that way.

## Third Grade of High School

In grade three, Golnaz and Rana were not in the same class as us anymore. It was just me, Yasaman, and Setareh. I got closer to Maryam, spending a lot of time at her house or she stayed at mine.

We had our own world. We were getting invited to parties and dating. I was dating Amir, a boy who we had met at the mall across the street from my house. Meeting other kids, having coffee, and just hanging out together was a lot of fun. In the mornings, we had little motivation to go to school.

Usually, Maryam stayed at my house because it was also closer to school. We would talk all night and sleep late. It was hard to wake up in the mornings.

Maryam was a rational girl and would discuss things from a realistic point of view. But she was also courageous and a risk taker as much as I was.

We had to get to school on time; otherwise, the door would be closed, and we would have to stand outside during the morning program. This was boring and made me anxious. We didn't know what punishment awaited us while walking toward the classrooms and being checked by the principals.

## A Forbidden Birthday Party

Yasaman always invited us to all her older brother Fazad's birthday parties. On this occasion, she and Faraz planned to invite all their friends and have a big party.

It was mid-October, and I was looking forward to the party. I had told my dad and had gotten permission three weeks before. At first, he had said that I could go, but I had to be back home by ten p.m. After a lot of explanation that 10 p.m. was too early, he reluctantly convinced me to be home before midnight. This was a breakthrough for me.

Prior to this, my dad believed that every girl had to be home before it got dark. And if I was invited anywhere, I had to be back before 10 p.m.

Yasaman's birthday was really fun. There were many boys and girls around the same age as me or a little older.

I had gone to the party with Amir, the guy I was dating at the time, and his friend. It was around 11:30 p.m. when I started to get anxious. I told Amir we had to leave, as I needed to get home before midnight, yet Yasaman and Farzad insisted we stay until he had blown out the candles and had cake. But I had to go. Otherwise, I knew I would have to deal with an angry father at home. So, we left.

As we were walking toward the end of the street, we saw three police cars racing toward the house. When they stopped in front of their building, it was obvious they were going in there because of the party. We were worried that somebody might stop us, too.

"They are going to be arrested," Amir said with a scared tone.

The next school day, none of my classmates, who had been at the party, were at school. I heard later that they had been arrested and taken to Vozara Jail. It was a police station where people who breached Islamic laws—for instance, wearing an incorrect hijab or were at a mixed boys and girls party—were taken.

It was a nasty jail. It was a place where they would also hold prostitutes, drug addicts, and others who had committed crimes. Basically, people who had been arrested at parties, or boys and girls who were not married caught together, were put in the same category. They would take them to Vozara until a judge charged them in an Islamic court weeks later. If they were lucky, they would only get a fine. Still, the hassle and mental challenge it would cause was severe.

The effect it had mentally, and the stress it caused people who were arrested and their families, was unbelievable. My friends were there, and they would have to stay in Vozara over the weekend. Their parents had to go back and forth until the end of April when they were to go to court and would be charged with their crimes and penalties.

Although, at the beginning, some parents got angry, I guess they later had no choice but to attend the court sessions with their children.

For those who had been arrested, it became a kind of fun activity. On the other hand, it was an opportunity for boys and girls to meet up and get to know each other. A lot of the time, there were other kids who we knew, and we would say hi to them. It was nice to see them!


## *Chaharshanbesoori*

A few days before the Iranian New Year, on March 20th, the last Tuesday night of the year is called Chaharshanbesoori, meaning Wednesday party. It is an old tradition rooted in ancient Zoroastrian Iranians.

The tradition is to jump from on top of the fire and read some poems, saying, "My yellow color for you, and your red color for me." This means becoming healthy, getting energy from the fire, and getting rid of any sickness and worries.

Children also go to neighbors' houses and knock on doors, asking for nuts and candy. It's similar to trick or treating at Halloween.

But, when we were in high school, this tradition had been changed and transformed into what had become a dangerous event. Young people, or sometimes even older ones, would buy explosives and make handmade grenades. When they exploded, it sounded like a mini-bomb explosion! Sometimes, the explosions were big, and the sound was much worse.

Every year around this time, there were programs on TV warning kids and youngsters about the dangers of playing with explosives. They would show photographs of kids who had severe burns or who had lost an eye while trying to make mini grenades in the basement of their houses. They hid the explosives and would go and play with them. But, because of the heat or contact with the material, they often exploded and caused so many injuries to children.

Did it make us, especially the boys, keep further away from these things? Well, I guess it worked for me because I wasn't really into playing with things like explosives. I was more excited about the day itself, going out and playing with other kids.

I was scared of explosives, but I can bravely say that Chaharshanbesoori was also one of the few exciting, fun events for teenagers around my age those days.

Everyone would come onto the street to play and party, turn the music up, and dance. They were always scared of the committee coming and arresting people. If they did, we had to run away. On our street, though, my mom stayed with me and my little brother and didn't leave us, which wasn't pleasant. We would rather have been left alone.

One of those days, after the morning program, we walked toward our classes silently, in lines, and then the teacher came in and started teaching physics. The only thing I could think about was killing time until the break that we had for twenty minutes … and then also the class after that, and basically the whole day.

I couldn't focus on the lessons. My thoughts were flying everywhere else, mostly occupied by anything other than studying.

We were sitting in absolute silence, and we could only hear the teacher's chalk on the blackboard as she wrote formulas when there was suddenly an explosion that shook the whole building. There was no time for anyone to wait or think. We all ran toward the hallway where we had seen some smoke.

Our friend, Mina, was lying on the ground, and there was a big, dark circle next to her from an exploded grenade. She had been naughty and had gotten the grenade from her boyfriend. She had wanted to throw it into the middle of all the students and scare them after school had finished.

This would happen a lot, with students or boys from schools nearby. As Mina had been running to her classroom, because it was getting late, she had slipped and fallen over, causing the grenade to explode. She was so shocked and scared that she couldn't get up and run before everyone else had arrived.

It was a strange scene and extremely funny. Mina stood up, and the principal dragged her to the office. The students laughed, and teachers tried to lead them back to their classrooms.

Because she was our friend, we were worried about what would happen to her and barely paid attention to the rest of our lessons that day. The next day, we heard she had been expelled from school.

We didn't realize what happened until later that summer when we met her again in summer school for failed grades. She explained that she begged the principal not to call her father and tell him the story because her father was suffering from heart disease. So, they had called her mother instead. But the next day, her father showed up at the school, and they told him the whole story.

Mina, who was really worried about her dad, slapped the principal's ear and so was expelled from the school immediately. They had let her take the summer classes, but she had to go to another school after that.

# CHAPTER 8

# Running Away from Home to Go Skiing

*Yearning to Ski*

It was a day in February when we heard that the main ski resort had opened for the winter season. I was extremely happy, even though I knew I would have to deal with asking permission from my father each time I wanted to go skiing. It wasn't going to be easy, but it was still worthwhile.

I guess, in those days, it was the only place where I could feel freedom for a few hours with no pressure from family, school, or the police in the street who worried about my hijab or me speaking to a guy.

Being a teen and having been kept away from boys in school and society, I found them to be such interesting creatures. I didn't have a clue what I was attracted to. Like any other teenager, I just wanted to get to know and hang out with them. But this was taboo in my country. It was against the law. You could be arrested. You could go to prison. Your parents had to get you out of jail, and it wasn't easy. It causes a lot of mental stress before they let someone go.

There were rumors that if a girl was arrested with a guy, they would send her to be seen and checked by government-verified doctors. And if she was not a virgin, she would be forced into Aghd (Islamic marriage).

I was anxious to ask my father whether I could go skiing. He never punished me physically, but his anger was not something that I wanted to face. He was not the type of father who swore or used improper words, but he would say, "Bad!

Go to your room!" He could flip in a matter of seconds, which made me constantly stressed when I was around him.

That night, when he came home and sat on the chair where he normally sat, next to the fireplace, I asked, "Dad, the ski resorts are open now. Can I go skiing this weekend?"

He looked at me from above his glasses and behind the newspaper and said in a serious tone, "You can only go skiing after you receive your first semester results."

That was like a sword right into my heart. It was the only thing I had been looking forward to for the past few months. I thought, Why? But why? Everything was such a challenge. It seemed that having fun was illegal, not only in my country but also in my home!

I didn't realize this during all those years I was a teenager, but I wondered, Isn't freedom the natural right of any human being? Okay, I am still young and don't know the dangers that could cause problems for any young girl my age. But why did we have to be so isolated?

So, where, apart from school and home, could we go? Was there a nightclub or a bar like everywhere else that young people could go to meet and have fun?

Such things didn't exist in Iran and still don't. There were house parties, but at that age, I was only allowed to go to girl parties and not mixed ones because of the danger of the committee coming and arresting us.

Years later, I understood that having discipline is fundamental in any household. In our house, there was a discipline that helped me in many aspects of my life. But what was the reason for such tough restrictions? Were my parents worried about us all the time in case the committee arrested us?

Even more than hanging around boys, their main concern was the committee. My father had told me that if I was arrested, I couldn't count on him to get me out of jail. This was only a threat, of course, but it was so real to me back then.

Sarah Tehrani

## *Running Away to Stay in the North*

My friends and I were upset that my parents would go to other cities in the north for the Persian New Year holidays in March. But we ended up going somewhere close to our friends with Maryam's parents and another family. Ana was about to become engaged to her boyfriend, Arvin, who was also with us. We were so excited and happy for them.

It was nice to be there, to meet up with other kids and hang out. However, we were not allowed to go to Khanedarya, the northern resort where we sometimes went for our holidays. We were a big group, but all we thought about was seeing our friends and other kids. The second week of the holidays was when all our friends were coming.

The environment in their house was friendly and stress-free. Her mom and dad would let them talk loudly, and they weren't worried about doing something wrong at their house.

One night, when we were all sleeping, I woke up to hear Maryam calling her dad in the middle of the night. "Dad, please bring me water." I couldn't believe this! I used to laugh about it and say how unbelievable it was. This would never happen in our house!

We asked her mom to extend our stay for a second week of the New Year holiday, but they couldn't. This was so sad, and because we were so immature and our heads were in the clouds, we decided to run away. I don't remember whose idea this was. I think it was probably mine. We were both serious and excited to make it happen.

Everyone packed and got ready to head back to Tehran. We knew it was pointless to ask again to stay, but we planned to escape and stay anyway. We were fearless of the consequences, only thinking about our goal and following our emotions. Our determination was so strong that we didn't hesitate for a second.

We left the villa with the adults. They planned to have lunch on the way back to Tehran, so we asked them to leave us at Izadshahr, a resort on the way, while they had lunch. We said we wanted to say goodbye to our friends, and they could pick us up later.

At first, Maryam's parents were hesitant, but they agreed. They dropped us off, and we went into the resort and waited for them to leave.

Then we went back to the security kiosk and asked for a piece of paper and a pen.

We left her parents a note saying, "Sorry, but we are going to stay here. Don't worry about us." That was it! Then we headed to the beach.

The feeling of freedom and adrenaline was intense. The joy that I experienced was extraordinary. It was a feeling of breaking through. The excitement and the sense of getting to do what we wanted.

We decided to continue to walk to the next resort from the beach so they wouldn't see us, and then we headed in the opposite direction to the Hyatt Hotel, which was located toward the western side of where we were.

Our friends and the resort we wanted to go to, were Khanedarya. We guessed Ladan's parents would go looking for us there and instead we went to the opposite direction.

We headed toward the road and got a taxi to the Hyatt Hotel. We were not scared. We were happy, excited, free … not even thinking of where we might sleep that night. We had no idea. However, I was anxious when I thought about my parents, so I tried not to think about them but rather let the joy of staying in the north.

We got to the Hyatt Hotel after an hour. Maryam called her grandma to assure her that we were okay. She was such a kind and knowledgeable lady. She laughed at us and said, "Your parents are really concerned and have asked the police to look for you. But don't worry; just stay safe. I will tell them you called." She also told Maryam, "Good for you that you did this. They should have listened to you."

That was a relief. At least someone was supportive.

I called my home, too. My mom sounded so worried when she asked where we would sleep that night. I replied that I didn't know yet. She said she would talk to my aunt and told us to return to Izadshahr and spend the night there. She said they would come to my grandparents' villa the next day.

We ordered two cafés glacé at the hotel's coffee shop and drank happily. Then, we got a taxi and headed back to Izadshahr where was my aunts villa, with great joy.

We went to my aunt's place and knocked on the door. She welcomed us, although her husband looked a little unwelcoming, even angry. But my aunt was nice and kind. She said, "Please stay here tonight till your mom and grandparents come tomorrow."

We were happy and left to meet up with friends at the beach. It was a great day. We were so happy that we had gotten to stay for a second week. We had no thoughts of what our parents had gone through, their concerns about two teenage girls being on their own in the north, that anything might have happened to us.

There were no mobile phones back then. I went to the shop in front of the resort entrance to call my mom. I called her again the next day. They had arrived at my grandparents' villa, which was fifty miles from where we were in the north.

My mom asked me to head to the villa. She wasn't angry, and I wasn't afraid, as my dad had not come with them. I knew that my grandparents would be kind, too. I knew there wouldn't be any concerns when we got there. So, we headed to Motelghoo to stay with them.

The second week was great. For a few days, we would head to Khanedarya in a taxi in the morning to meet up with friends and then go back home at night. Even though it was a three-hour drive, it was worth it.

I was barely doing any studying and didn't have the motivation to do so. It was because, for the final exams, we either tried to cheat or handed in our papers without writing anything on them. I think it was a sort of protest to the situation.

## Dating

I had no sense of understanding or figuring out the social class or educational level of people. Then, the only important thing was how cool and popular or good-looking guys were. After dating Amir, however, I eventually realized he wasn't the right fit for me.

One day, I got into a fight with him after he chased us when we returned from a friend's house because I hadn't told him where I was going.

Then I met another guy, and we thought we were in love. He was quite good-looking, but we were never intimate. We didn't even have anywhere to go other than the coffee shops. Even if the coffee shops were busy, we couldn't hold hands. But he had become friends with one of the local drivers and would pay him to take us around in his car so we could sit in the back and hold hands without fear of the committee seeing us.

We dated for almost nine months, thinking immaturely that we were the right fit for each other. We wanted to get married so that we could at least go to places in public easily.

Another place we would go to often was a hiking area in mountains called Darake. It was the place to go, especially on Thursdays during the summer. It would be packed by young teenagers like us who would hike all the way to the top and then gather in a few of the restaurants on the way. Some people used to jump in the river from the big rock. But when we went there, we were always scared of getting caught by the committee.

One day, my mom stalked us as I waited at a street junction for him to pick me up in his taxi driver friend's car. When they came, I got into the car, and we kept going toward the southern part of the city and areas that weren't nice or considered as safe as the northern part ... which was when my mom lost us.

When I got back home, Dad wanted to talk with me in his office. He asked where I had been for the past few hours. I said I had been waiting to meet my friend, Yasaman. He told me not to lie and said he knew I'd gotten into a red car. He wanted me to explain who the person was in the car and where we went.

So, I told him in detail, but with such fear that I was shivering. I explained that I loved this guy, and we wanted to get married. I wasn't even eighteen, but together, we had decided to marry each other so we could have a life getting to at least communicate with each other. That was the only level of interaction that I could have with boys in my young world.

My boyfriend said he was ready to come to our house and talk to my mom. When my mom shared this with my dad, he refused to be there and didn't take any of it seriously. So, his mom came alone with a small, cheap bucket of flowers. Even though I didn't care about these sorts of things, it caught my attention right away.

His mom and my mom, had a long conversation, and she told us that it was fine. We could become engaged and wear rings so that we could go around without being interrupted by committee members. That was such a relief!

I assume they had also decided that we were so young that this could give us the freedom to figure things out ourselves. Obviously, our parents had recognized how childish and immature we still were, and they wanted to find a way for us to pass this stage and find the right reason for our persistence to get married. It turned out to be the right action.

We went to buy the rings during the next few days. Then we wore them and told everyone we were engaged.

I loved the feeling of freedom more than I loved him. We could go hiking and hold hands in the crowd.

A couple of times, the committee asked about our relationship. We could reply with such confidence, telling them we were engaged and showing them our rings. That was amazing!

After about a month, I began to feel that I didn't agree with many things about this guy. I began to realize that I didn't really love him that much. Then, after making excuses, one day, I broke up with him and gave him his ring back.

## Rebellious Behavior

I was drawn toward a group of friends at high school who were considered to be rebellious.

I started to stay away from home, as I couldn't bear my dad's pressure or anything about home. The last thing I cared about was school. I still kept going, but I had failed so many lessons that I would have to retake them. My mom kept scheduling teachers to help me, and Dad paid for so many private sessions.

Thankfully, I never had to retake a full year, but grades three and four were the worst of my score history. I was so disinterested that when one physics teacher used to come, I would ask her to sit down, and then I'd go to my brother's room next door and close my eyes for five minutes to rest. Then, I'd go back to the room where she was waiting to continue teaching.

The summer after the third grade was the most difficult. I hardly ever had a full night's sleep, as I had to retake seven modules, almost all of the main ones, even religious study.

Almost all of the papers I handed in were blank at the end-of-the-year exams, and I got a zero score.

It had become a joke to study, and my parents had to really work hard for that. The school held classes that students who had failed could take. It gave us one more chance to take the final exams, as well as the scheduled September retake exam dates.

I skipped classes here and there to go hiking with friends. During one of the hikes, we were caught by the committee because we were with boys.

My friends ran away, but I kept talking to the sister who was with the committee brothers. I cried all the way down the hills and begged them to let me go. When they caught me, one of the brothers showed me his gun, and I was scared to run.

In the end, after a few hours, they let me go. But they got my friend's diary and her phone number, and they called all the numbers in the diary to find her.

## *Banned from Classes*

The day that I went to school to register for the July classes, the principal, Farhadi, stopped me and remarked that I had plucked my eyebrows and said that I wouldn't be able to attend the July classes. She was the same one who had told me when I was in the first grade that I could be the ambassador of the class, and I had refused.

My mom went to the school and asked her a few times if I could stay in the summer classes. She explained that it was vital for me to study and said that those classes would really help me. But the principal said the decision had been made, and I would have to take all seven exams in September. I couldn't believe what she was saying, especially because my eyebrows were so light and not full. I might have learned to pluck out a few, but it was not completely done.

The next day, my mom went to the school again to talk to her, yet she was firm. They wouldn't let me take those classes.

For my mom, who had always been a top student, it was hard to accept that her daughter didn't study. She would tell me that sometimes and express her disappointment.

Dad didn't interfere much, but he was not happy about this, either.

I had teachers for all the seven modules that came and went after each other, even for religious studies and Arabic. On the night of the exams, I slept for a couple of hours and studied hard. I had not studied anything for a year. Even though I had no interest in the lessons, I still tried to pass the grades. The concept of repeating the year was out of the question and unacceptable I did whatever I could to pass during the exams, which lasted about fifteen days. Eventually, I passed all seven modules and was promoted to the fourth grade

# PART III

## Escape, Freedom, Stress, and Prison

# CHAPTER 9

# My Last Year of High School

## *My Parents' Concern*

I had started school one year early, so I was not yet eighteen when I started my last year of high school. Nevertheless, I felt pretty grown up and wanted the right to do many things.

This was when my parents started to become more concerned about me.

My dad had asked my cousin, to look after me. He wanted her to take me out and introduce me to her friends so they had some control. Of course, I wasn't aware of this, and I was more than happy to hang out with Neda and her group of friends who were older than me, in their mid-twenties, and were considered cool guys.

Neda my cousin, was six years older than me, and her boyfriend, Shahab, was about the same age. They hung out a lot, having fun socializing.

Shahab was an artist, and his father was a well-known singer who had left Iran to live in the U.S. after the revolution. Shahab had a great voice and played piano without printed sheet music when he heard any songs he knew. It was fun to go to their social gatherings and sing with others when they played the piano or other instruments. This made their group of friends so much fun, and so I started going to their gatherings with Neda.

Two brothers, Peyman and Bardia, had their apartment in the same building as their parents. Their late father had been a close friend of my dad's before he married my mom. We found out about this later on. Their father had died in a car crash. Their mother, was Miss Iran in the 1970s.

She had remarried, and their stepfather was a kind man who was always nice to us when we were their guests.

They were great horse riders. There were a few couples, and it was quite entertaining. We laughed, played, joked a lot, and had great times. They all treated me like their little sister and cared for me. They took me horse riding with them, and I was glad to have finally found cool, fun friends who were also acceptable to my parents, thanks to my cousin.

After I had been to their house a few times, I began to fancy the younger brother, Peyman. He was quite handsome. We would talk once in a while, but we didn't date. He seemed quite confused about what he wanted with me.

Meanwhile, I started dating another friend of Neda's boyfriend, who was eleven years older than me and was an actor. Neda wasn't happy about that and hadn't talked to me for a few months. Of course, I was barely in a relationship with the guy. He worked in another town, filming, and called me from a public phone at nine p.m. every night. That was almost all our relationship entailed, though we went to a couple of parties together when he was in town.

One night, we were invited to a friend's birthday party. My cousin said she wasn't going and would stay with me at our house. I insisted on going, however, and we planned that the guy I was dating would pick me up at 10:30 p.m. after everybody had gone to bed. My cousin said she would cover for me so I could go and come back without anyone knowing.

Of course, there were no mobile phones back then, so when he called and said, "Honey, I will pick you up in thirty minutes," my dad, who we thought had already gone to bed, picked up the phone from his office downstairs and heard our conversation.

As I opened the door to get out of the house, dressed up and wearing makeup, my dad stood in his pajamas, staring at me. I was so scared and shocked that I shut the door and locked it out of fear.

Both Neda and I were shaking, and she was swearing at me in whispers. I never got to go out that night, and my dad didn't say a word. Still, I was afraid to face him for a few days. There was no way to let the guy know I couldn't get out, so that relationship ended soon afterward.

Then two new people, a sister and brother, started to hang out with my cousin's friends. The guy was called Abtin, and his sister was Samira.

They were fun. Both of them were studying at well-known universities and were welcome in the group.

## *Meeting Abtin*

Start Here

Abtin was a big drinker, and he was a clown who made everyone laugh all the time. He was good-looking, too. At the time, one of the guys from the group had started dating my close classmate and friend, Yasaman.

Yasaman's boyfriend, Arvin, used to play persian tar, and he had a great voice. They had been dating for almost a year when we planned to have lunch at Dizzy Sara. This traditional restaurant only served Iranian traditional meat stew, which I didn't like back then.

Abtin came to have lunch with us. There were just a few of us. I asked them to get me a hot dog from a supermarket down the road called Super Jordan. I couldn't stand the smell and taste of dizi. Abtin kept making jokes about how I could I don't like Dizzy. He thought it was unbelievable that I had never tried raw onion. We laughed a lot. It was a fun day, and I ended up having a little of the meat stew that I found out I didn't hate it that much!

Abtin asked me for my number so we could talk some more. I didn't even know if I liked him, but it was as if I had to do this. He was twenty-five years old, studying computer science and working in the same field, so I found him eligible for dating.

He lived in a nice house, and his sister, Sami, was beautiful and kind. His mother was always grumpy and would look skeptical when she looked at me, making me uncomfortable. I never met his father, who was separated from his mom. His mom, was a breast cancer survivor, so they were careful not to bother her and to follow her rules.

Abtin had recently broken up with his ex-girlfriend, who had friends in our group. He asked me if he could be my boyfriend after we had talked on the phone a few times and met. I liked the idea. After all, he was a cool guy, educated, good-looking, and welcomed into the group, and I was happy to be seen with him. That was my definition of love at that age. But did I love him? I don't think so. I just wanted to have a boyfriend different from the guys I had previously dated.

We started going out with each other, hanging out with the group, and having a great time. We were intimate, which was also something new to me. Also, I soon realized that Abtin's father was an opium smoker, which was why his parents were separated. Although his family was comfortable and lived in a nice house in a nice area, Abtin didn't have much money. If he was lucky, his dad would lend him their beige Cadillac, and we would go out to dinner. Otherwise, he would drive the beat-up pickup truck from his dad's work.

When you looked at the truck from the front, it looked crooked and seemed to be approaching you at an angle. My friends used to laugh hard at this. I never cared about his car or how much he would spend on me. It didn't matter because my parents had taught me that being a good human mattered most. Material wealth would not guarantee happiness and prosperity in life. Deep down, I was convinced he was a good person, although he didn't always have the best attitude.

We used to go out for dinner together, but I had to pay for my share most of the time. He loved spicy food, so we used to go to an Indian restaurant in the center of town a lot.

# CHAPTER 10

## University

### *Abtin and The Bad Relationship*

In my first year at the University, Abtin started his compulsory military service. For the first three months, he attended training in a town far from Tehran, which was quite cold. After forty-five days, He lost so much weight when he got back for the first time that it was hard to recognize him.

Apparently, the food was so bad, and the way it was prepared was even worse, that he could barely eat anything except canned tuna and bread. He was lucky that, as an educated soldier, he could work around the kitchen. As a result, he had many stories to share.

One story was about the chef boiling water in a big pot, and many flies were in the kitchen. As he held the lid up to add ingredients, the steam got to the flies, and they fell into the pot. He carried on cooking the food with the flies in it and would never touch it himself. When he returned to town, we would spend time with our friends. We went horse riding or sometimes went out of town for the weekends.

Mostly, I felt left out of the group of friends because Neda and her friends were older and usually discussed topics I didn't know about or people I had never met.

Milad's girlfriend was best friends with Abtin's ex, and most of the time, she didn't include me in conversations about the past or the memories they shared.

Abtin also had another friend called Arezou. She was a funny girl who looked and behaved like a boy. Everybody loved her, but she didn't talk to me much. She was close to Abtin, and they would hang out and spend hours talking.

Arezou lived in England, she used to visit Iran quite often. Arezou's and Abtin's parents were good friends, too, and we used to go to their house in the summer and spend time at the pool when she was in town.

## The Conquer

Everyone was getting ready for the university exam acceptance test called The Conquer. My only interest was in the English language so I could get out of the country one day, but my dad repeatedly refused the idea. He said once that maybe I could leave after I got my bachelor's degree and finished university.

We could only choose English as the first choice, not the second or third. Therefore, my second choice was French, my third was German, and my fourth was Italian language. We could also tick a box so they pick a fifth option for us if we weren't accepted in our own subject choices.

We were asked where we wanted to study. My choices were all in Tehran, and I had ticked the box for a fifth city of their choice if I wasn't accepted for any of the four.

When the results came out, I doubted if I had been accepted because I had barely practiced the test or studied.

Our house phone rang. It was our neighbor's son, who was also attending the national Conquer for university that year. My mom answered, and he had told her, "Congratulations! Sarah has been accepted. Her name is in the newspaper."

My mom called me from the kitchen, "Sarah, Soroush says you've been accepted, and your name is in the newspaper."

"Really?" I said, surprised. I somehow doubted it and thought that it might be a mistake.

Then he stopped by to show me the newspaper.

I was happy that I had been accepted, although I was not happy that I had to study in the city they had chosen for me. It wasn't in Tehran and wasn't any of my choices. It was in Roudehen, a town one hour away, in the Alborz mountain range. It is en route to the northern part of Iran.

The good thing was that I had been accepted for a Bachelor of English Language Translation, which I preferred more than the other languages. My parents seemed pleased, although not satisfied.

## *Introduction to University*

The University of Roudehen did not have a good reputation. The reason, of course, was mostly because the students who stayed in the dormitory would hang out in the religious town.

At the university, they were strict. You had to wear a chador, the black cover over our normal hijab, with a scarf and manteaux. It was compulsory. I went there with my mom on enrollment day. I didn't like the atmosphere at all, and everything made me anxious.

They checked my nails at the sisters' entrance to make sure I wasn't wearing nail polish, that my hijab was covering my face properly, that there was no hair sticking out, and had no makeup.

The sisters' entrance was on a separate street from the brothers', where it went into a large building alongside a smaller building. The building where we had our classes was newer. There were five classrooms and offices and a big eating area on the lower ground floor, which overlooked the valley behind it. The smaller building, closer to the brothers' entrance, also had a food area and five floors of classrooms and offices.

The first day that I arrived for registration, I had mixed feelings. I was excited but unhappy because I didn't see any familiar faces of the people I knew in Tehran. It looked like this crowd of students was from a different part of the city.

I had to register for the transportation service to take me to the university. I was not allowed to drive there, and I didn't have a car.

On the first day of classes, my mom took me to where the autobus stops at 5:30 a.m. We left for the university shortly afterward.

Students were having fun on the autobus. They talked to the driver, turned on the music, and made jokes. Meanwhile, I was mostly nauseous because of my motion sickness. I didn't realize why then, but I was getting dizzy talking to people when I turned my head. That went on for one hour of driving.

I couldn't relate to their music, which was mostly recent Iranian songs. I used to listen to Guns' n Roses or other older Iranian songs, not these.

I soon became friends with a girl called Marjan, who lived in the upper part of Tehran. We could at least talk about the same topics. Another girl that I became friends with used to wear a strict hijab. Her name was Rahele. She was from a religious family, we connected and sat next to each other in class, on the bus, or went to the canteen together.

What I knew I should do was to finish this course and graduate, even though I did not enjoy the environment at all. Some of our professors were religious people who wore the aba and amame. They taught religious studies or a course called Imam Khomeini's Will that was compulsory to take.

## Unpopular Students and Personal Isolation

I didn't like university at all.

I don't know if I was too introspective, but I felt isolated from my relationship with Abtin during those years. I wasn't happy about everything going on at home with my parents and not being close to them. After that horrible high-school experiment, after turning eighteen, I felt more mature, but I was not happy in general. Most nights, I cried before I fell asleep. Crying made me feel calm.

There was a café in the university town, which was popular for students to go and have breakfast before class. Soon, we learned about it and went there to eat in the morning or have lunch. They had locally baked fresh bread, eggs, and milk, which were delicious. It was usually quite crowded, with most tables full.

The weather in the mountains was crisp and cold, which was nice, and I soon got used to getting up early to get there. Also, going to the café was something to look forward to.

I made a few other friends who I didn't get close to any of them, except Hale, a fun girl. We laughed a lot during those days and usually at silly topics.

A few times, people in the town said harsh words to us, or they would swear at us and tell us to leave their town. Initially, I didn't understand why, but then I realized that the town was highly religious. The students were apparently changing the local culture, and this is what people didn't appreciate.

In my second year, I sometimes took my mom's car to university. But the drive was dangerous up and down the mountains with all the heavy trucks. There were a lot of really bad accidents involving students who drove to university, and a lot of them were badly injured or killed. I was nervous and would be completely focused on the road when I drove. Usually, I had to return home by a set time, my mom was okay to give me her car once a week. My dad didn't let me drive under any circumstances, even though I had my driver's license.

Driving out of the town gave me so much pleasure. It was as if I were running away from everything happening. It gave me so much peace to listen to music and watch everything around me, especially when I drove along the highway that linked the city to the road in the mountains.

I loved the early mornings and the freedom that I felt. I liked what I was learning, as well. English literature and Poetry, linguistics, translation methodology, and so on were all interesting. I enjoyed the subjects. I passed two years and was getting full modules with twenty-four credits each term. This helped me to finish the bachelor's program quickly, in three-and-a-half years instead of four.

## *A Volatile Relationship*

My relationship with Abtin was almost two years old. However, it was volatile by the time I was in my last year of university. He was rude toward me without me really understanding it, and I was always needy and upset. Still, that wasn't what I had hoped for. It was as if my world revolved around our relationship.

The cultural influence was so great because it was my first intimate relationship. I could not imagine any other person coming into my life, even though my family was not religious. Maybe a lot of girls at the time felt the same about their first relationship with a guy, and this was the influence of my culture.

I was always nervous when waiting for him to call me and plan something. I also kept breaking up with him over and over again. Then, I would call him to apologize.

One time, when we had broken up, Maryam and I drove to his house, and I rang the bell. He answered and said, "Come up." He was happy to see me. I was so emotionally drained that I felt dizzy and was about to fall down when he held me. I didn't even realize what had happened, but when I became aware of my surroundings, I saw that he looked a bit angry. He said, "You should go. My mom is arriving soon."

His mom had told him a few times to be careful with me and not to break my heart. He used to joke about it and tell me what she had said. His sister, Sami, sometimes talked to me and asked me if everything was going well between us.

We would hang out with the same group of friends, although I still felt left out, especially when they all got drunk, joked around, and laughed. But there were a lot of fun times, too.

What I hated the most was that he smoked opium, like his dad. One day, when his mom was out, he smoked beside their fireplace. The smell was disgusting, and the act of doing it traumatized me. However, I didn't let him see that in my face and acted as if everything was fine.

Another time, he told me to go to his friend's house. The friend's parents were away, and they were going to all smoke together. The host's girlfriend and I were there, too.

They all lay down on the floor with their tools for smoking Opium. As they smoked, they seemed high and talked about their fantasies. They offered me a smoke, but I politely refused. Thankfully, nobody insisted. I was even more disgusted in this environment, but somehow, I kept thinking that he was my boyfriend and that it was all okay.

Being exposed to this freaked me out, I didn't tell anybody. I just kept it secret.

# CHAPTER 11

## The Trip to Shiraz and Other Adventures

### *Holiday with Boyfriend*

I got permission from my parents to go on a trip to Shiraz with friends. I believed that my dad thought I was with my girlfriends. I wasn't sure whether my mom was sharing everything with him, including that she knew my boyfriend was with me on that trip.

Bardia and his girlfriend, Abtin and I, and two other friends, Yasmin and Arezou, went on the trip. It is one of the most historical towns in Iran, where poets like Hafiz lived. We got three rooms, one for us girls and two for the boys, and we would switch them at night because unmarried couples were not allowed to stay in the same room.

Again, throughout most of the trip, I was not included in their conversations, jokes, or plans. I guess I was too young. I don't think the girls wanted to include me, either. It may or may not have been intentional. It's a question that I can't answer, but the boys would follow them.

It was as if I was a toddler who should go to bed at night. Abtin and I would say goodbye and then go back to our room. We lay there, and before I fell asleep, he would get up, thinking I was asleep, and go back to the other room to hang out with the rest. I was so upset that I would cry myself to sleep.

The trip was the most upsetting one that I had ever been on. A bump formed on the side of my neck when we got there. My mom took me to the doctor, and they said it was a lymph node infection, probably from a cold or stress.

Abtin had started a company with a friend who had become his partner. They did architectural plot drawings on a computer and printed them on special machines. I used to get him lunch and drop it off at his office sometimes. He was always busy, so we couldn't talk much, and I wouldn't call his office often. He also had plans to leave Iran and would talk about going to the U.S. occasionally.

## When Parents Were Away

Maryam was also dating a guy. He was called Dara and was the same age as Abtin. Abtin and Dara knew each other, too. He was in med school to become a doctor, and he was a handsome guy who seemed really in love with Maryam.

My parents were going to the north for a holiday, and I asked them if I could stay with Maryam at her house. I had plans.

I made copies of the keys for our front door, the security door over it, and the entrance door so we could get back to the house and Abtin and Dara could stay there with us.

When my parents left, we returned to the house with Maryam, Abtin, and Dara. We had so much fun for three days. We had breakfast together. Then they went to work, and after returning, we ordered food and watched movies. With Maryam we watched the movie Titanic thirteen times in a few days.

I called my mom and told her it was all good at Maryam's house. On the last day, I cleaned up as much as possible and put everything back as it was. Our neighbor's daughter, Noushin, who was my friend, knew I was at home, and she brought a kebab and rice for us. I left it in the microwave to warm it up but totally forgot about it. We cleaned, emptied the trash, locked the doors, and left the house.

When my parents came back, my mom found the bowl of rice and kebab in the microwave. Of course, they realized we had broken into the house, and I was told off severely.

My relationship with Abtin was rocky, as he was a social butterfly, always finding any excuse to laugh and have fun. Recently, it hit me that I didn't like how he behaved and was always ashamed him being drunk. The main thing hurting me was that I wanted him to be romantic. I was thinking of him as my love, of course, would never get the same feeling back from him.

Many times, I cried and called it off. Again, I called him back, and we talked. This went on until the end of the second year.

One time that we broke up, I got so sick that I went to the hospital and had to stay there, as they put me on an intravenous drip. I was so weak and tired.

Maryam called him and told him that I was sick, and he came to visit me. He stayed for a short time and left so quickly that I felt even more hurt.

## *Misadventure to Shemshak*

My friend Mina's dad had gotten her a brand-new Renault for her birthday. She asked us to go to the ski resort in the mountains. Mina, another friend, Sahar, and I headed toward Shemshak in her new black Renault. Abtin and his friend, Bardia, were supposed to come a little later.

We sang in the car and drank a cocktail that they made with vodka. I was lying in the back and looking at the sky and mountains, thinking how beautiful they were. I was also thinking about my relationship with Abtin and wondering why it was such hard work, when my friends said, "Come on, Sarah. Don't sleep back there. We are nearly there."

I sat up, wearing my sunglasses, and we all happily sang. A few minutes later, close to a restaurant called Koohestan, where the road was narrow and near the top of the mountain, a car came out of its lane to pass another car and crashed head-on into our car. My face smashed onto the front seat. I felt some pain, but then it mostly went numb.

Mina and Sahar exited the car, screaming at the other driver, "What are you doing? Didn't you see us?"

I looked down, and there was blood everywhere. When Mina and Sahar noticed, they started screaming even louder. "Look what you did to our friend. Her nose is broken!" They completely panicked. "Oh my God, what should we do?"

Everyone kind of forgot about the accident, looking for someone to take me back to Tehran and to the hospital.

After a few minutes had passed, Abtin and Bardia arrived. Abtin took me back, and Bardia stayed with my friends to help them with the police report and the crash paperwork.

Abtin was so angry with me. I didn't feel anything. I'm not sure if it was because of the shock of the crash or because of the vodka that we had been drinking. Also, my nose was not that painful.

He told me that I should call my mom to come to the hospital because he couldn't stay there with me. We called my mom, and I told her I was okay, but my nose was broken. She said I should go to Iranmehr Hospital because my grandfather had a doctor friend there that they had served in the army together.

My mom came, and Abtin told her he had to leave immediately. She looked quite worried for me. We had to wait for the doctor, so they prepared me for surgery.

I went to the toilet, and that was when I saw my nose was not in its right place and my face was black and swollen.

Dr. Sajjadi was nice. Before the surgery, I asked her not to do any plastic jobs or change how my nose looked. I was so naïve to say that, but I hated the nose jobs that were common with girls back then. Dr. Sajjadi smiled and told me not to worry.

I was discharged the next day with my nose in a cast. Mina's car was totaled and couldn't be driven, so they had to sell it for a much lower price. Abtin was talking about leaving Iran and moving to the U.S. Our relationship was even more than rocky.

# CHAPTER 12

## Stopped by the Committee

### *Face-to-Face with the Committee*

I had just gotten my new driver's license and begged Mom to lend me her car, so Maryam and I could go to a shoe shop we regularly visit to see their new collection. They had nice, handmade boots that we bought all the time, even though they were expensive. I already owned a pair, we were waiting for the new styles to come out so we could replace our old ones.

The shop was in Asia Passage, which was located on Jordan Street. The street was popular for young people who would drive their cars and share phone numbers with others. We had no intention of going there for this reason, that they though.

There was also a popular coffee shop there. The best thing on their menu was "Ice Cream, Cream, and Chocolate." It was amazingly delicious. So, that day, we also went to Asia Passage to have one of those shakes.

My mom had told me to be back within two hours by 6.30 p.m., so we were in a rush to drive back after we had finished shopping. We got into my mother's car, and as I drove along Jordan Street, there was a lot of traffic, committee people, and military soldiers stopping cars on the side of the street.

We didn't get a chance to talk or do anything as one of them waved his hand and signalled for me to stop the car. I pulled over, one of the committees opened the door. We sat in the car, scared and surprised, staring at them.

A sister got into the back of the car. We used to call them Zeinab sisters. They were ladies who worked in the committee, guiding people to be good and taking action to stop them from doing anything that was forbidden by our religion.

I started crying, even though I still didn't know what would happen next. Usually, I thought, in these situations, you had to beg so they might feel sympathy and let you go ... or that was the only way out that I knew might work. But, for God's sake, we hadn't even been talking to a boy! It was just us two girls, with no makeup, with our Islamic hijab, driving down the street. What mistake had we made?

The Zeinab sister had a piece of paper and a pen in her hands. She looked at us and started writing something on a form. "Please let us go," I begged. "What have we done? We went to the shoe shop and now are going back home."

"You'll find out soon," she said seriously. Then, after a few moments of silence, she said, "Your crime is having makeup on, not wearing your hijab right, and wearing forbidden sunglasses."

We were in disbelief at the crime that we had supposedly committed and how everything had happened so fast.

As these thoughts passed through my mind with anger, I was imagining my father's face and how I could even deal with this, wishing they would let us go any second. Or maybe they would just give us a warning but the sister got out, and a young soldier entered the car.


## Temporary Prison

The soldier in the back of our car said, "Let's go." "Where to?" I asked in a voice that was near to tears. I was worried about my mom, who was expecting, and my dad, who would get angry with me. They would also be concerned and would think I'd had an accident. It was already 6:30!

"We are going to Vozara," the soldier answered.

While I was crying I told him, "My mom and dad are expecting us to be home already, so they will be concerned." However, I kept driving toward Vozara, crying and begging him to let us go.

Finally, the young soldier said, "Throw out all of your cassettes because they will search your car there. I can let your friend go because the sister has only filled in one form, but I can't do anything else."

I was still so happy that Maryam could go. Her mom would also have gotten so angry and upset, which would have been even more drama for all of us.

She exited the car in the middle of the road and left with all the cassettes.

When we got to Vozara, they opened the parking lot gate. My eyes were full of tears, and I was terribly anxious about what would happen next. I was so worried for my parents as I drove into the parking area.

They asked me to park the car and then follow them. We went into the basement, divided into different rooms with doors and a small window above each one. It was dark and damp. Close to the entrance, I met a sister and another girl who looked like a prostitute. She had heavy makeup on and was chewing gum loudly. I think she was also a resident there and was helping them. It looked as if she had been there for a long time. She wasn't inside the rooms but walking about freely. They were asking her to do things.

She pointed to another room and told me to go there. I felt nauseous.

I begged them to let me call my mom. "She is going to have a heart attack."

The sister shouted, "No. Go into the room right now!"

I went into the room crying. The room was filled with about fifteen other women and girls. Some of them looked calm, and some were worried and looked upset. I think I was one of the worst affected because I kept crying.

After about fifteen minutes, nobody was talking to anybody, or, if they did, it was brief questions like, "Do you know if they want to keep us here tonight?"

A sister opened the door. I went to the front, even though I was scared she would shout at me, and asked her if I could please call home. I told her my parents would be so worried by now because I was supposed to be home an hour ago.

"Follow me," she said.

I followed her, and she showed me a black phone hanging on the wall. "You can call from this phone."

Shakingly, I picked up the phone and called home. My mom answered, and I could tell that she was worried.

"Where are you, Sarah?" "I am in Vozara."

"What? Why?" she asked in shock.

"I was with Maryam when the committee stopped the car, and they brought me here. They let Maryam go, I asked her not to call you. She should be at her home by now."

My mom was silent. I can feel now, as a mother, how she must have felt hearing that her daughter had been arrested and was in jail.

They didn't let me finish the conversation and told me to return to the room, I felt relieved because at least my parents knew where I was. After about an hour, the same sister opened the door and called my name. She said, "Write down the number of your house."

They had called home and asked my parents to bring the house deed so that they could release me until we went to court.

My mom arrived around ten p.m., left the deed of our house with them, and they let her take me home. I had cried so much and been so anxious that I was exhausted. I also didn't want to deal with my dad. I was so worried.

But when we arrived home, my dad was surprisingly quiet. In general, he was a quiet man and would get quieter when he was angry. You could see the rage in his eyes, which was worse than any loud voice. Still, it was different this time. I think, deep down, he was happy that I had gotten back home safely and was relieved that his daughter didn't have to spend the night in jail.

I heard from my mom that he didn't believe they had stopped us just because of make up. He thought maybe there had been a boy in the car with us.

They had moved my mom's car to a bigger parking area, and on the fourth day, they gave us the paperwork, which included a description of my "crime," so we could go to court in a week.

## *Court Appearance*

Next day, we arrived at the court early. There were all sorts of cases, from satellite dishes that they had collected from someone's house to a lady who was complaining about her husband cheating on her. We had to wait almost three hours until it was our turn.

I went into the room with my mom. The judge didn't look into our eyes and looked a little disgusted talking to us. I don't know why, but it's probably because of how we were wearing our hijabs.

He looked at the paperwork, took some notes, and said, "You should pay this fine to get the car back."

My mom looked at the paper and then showed it to me. For each of my "crimes," there was a separate penalty. The total that we had to pay was approximately one 15,000 Toomans. Back then twenty years ago, it was a considerable amount.

My biggest concern was that my mom would get her car back because she depended on it. It was as if the worst thing had happened, and she wouldn't have her car for a few days. I guess it was her way of getting to my grandparents' house daily.

My grandma would nurture her, make her lunch, listen to her daily problems, or joke around. It was such a loving and warm environment that I think we were all addicted to going there.

We paid the penalty and were ready to get the car back. However, they told us that we needed to get a parking release from the head of Vozara. So, we had to go back from the court to Vozara. When we arrived, they said we should return tomorrow—the head of Vozara had gone for the day. The next day, we waited all day, but he didn't show up.

On the third day, we stood outside with a few other parents, waiting for them to call me. Then somebody did call my name! I followed her, scared and tense. We went upstairs to the head office. I knocked, and he told us to enter.

He was a short, middle-aged man. I had my scarf pulled over my forehead and was looking down to make sure I didn't do anything wrong. I just wanted this nightmare to be over.

He smiled and said, "Come in." Then he told me, "Look at the flag of Iran. Which color do you think is the nicest?"

I was confused and afraid to answer. I looked at the flag and said, "Green?"

"No, he said. "White is the best colour, and then you girls go and make yourselves up."

I didn't understand what he meant, but I said, "I am sorry, sir."

He stamped the parking ticket.

I grabbed it, turned back, and said, "Thank you." Then I shut the door, quickly went down the stairs, and got out of there.

The emotional distress that I had experienced over the past five to six days since I had been arrested was so intense that I felt exhausted. I just wanted to rest and didn't want to see anyone.

We went to the parking area, got my mom's car, and returned home. I slept the whole day after that, but I was still sad and worried. Dealing with that tension was incomprehensible to me.

In my youth, I couldn't understand why we had to go through this kind of punishment. Why did my family have to experience all this? It was all too much to handle.

# PART IV

## One Last Time

# CHAPTER 13

## The Relationship Deteriorates

### *An Uncertain Future*

My relationship with Abtin mostly entailed arguing and hanging up the phone when we talked to each other. He was rude, and I was stressed out. But we would still have dinner together and see our friends.

They had gatherings where everyone played different musical instruments, and a few would sing a classical persian song. Those were quite nice. Shahab played the piano, Arvin played the Iranian tar, and Arman played the guitar. They all sang. We had drinks and sang songs with them.

I wasn't satisfied with anything about the relationship. I felt as if I could cry at any second. I didn't understand what was wrong with me, but I knew it had something to do with the relationship.

Abtin kept talking about leaving the country and going to Dubai to get a U.S. visa so he could eventually move there, as they had extended family there.

The future of our relationship was vague and uncertain to me. I didn't know what would happen to us after almost two years together. I learned that a relationship should move to a more serious stage after a few years. I didn't dare to ask him, either. Instead, I was always upset and kept fighting with him over stupid matters, and I was needy.

One night in April, we went to friends' house, a sister and brother called Yasmin and Farid. When they had friends over, their parents were always cool, and they Would hang around with us kids and cook in the kitchen. A few of us were there that night, maybe around eight or nine people.

Yasmin was the same friend who had accompanied us on the Shiraz trip. She was nice and friendly. Farid, who had a serious girlfriend, Tara, was there, too.

We were all sitting in the kitchen. We were sitting around the table alking when this handsome, tall guy came in. He had such amazing energy that I couldn't help staring for a few seconds until I became aware I was. It was strange to me that I felt that way.

I listened to what he said as he was talking about the ski that day. From his face, you could tell that he had been skiing quite a lot because he was sunburned and he was quite athletic.

When we finished dinner, I got up and headed toward the trash can to empty the uneaten food from my plate. He was there, too. My heart started pounding, and my breathing became difficult. I was confused. I was so attracted to him that I worried someone might realise it from my face.

When we left that night, I realised his name was Roozbeh. However, I was so involved with my relationship with Abtin that I quickly forgot about it.

We kept arguing and fighting over small matters so much. It was mostly drama. I would hang up the phone on him at least once or twice a week. I would tell him I was done and couldn't tolerate it any longer. It was as if I were under more stress when I was not talking to him … as if something was missing.

Nothing could keep me happy except talking to him again. I wasn't enjoying anything at home or with my friends.

I spent a lot of time with Maryam at her house or our house. Still, we were attending different universities and, therefore, were busy with our schedules.

I was barely studying, but only because I liked the English language a lot and didn't need to. I enjoyed poetry and linguistics, although I found the rest of the classes boring. I would count the minutes to when I could get back on the bus or into my mom's car and head back to Tehran. I think it was around that time that we had our mobile phones, and I was mostly waiting to talk to Abtin.

# CHAPTER 14

## I Knew it was the End

### The End of a Relationship

We went to dinner at our favourite Indian restaurant. Afterwards, he dropped me off at home. We had barely talked on the way back. However, as I exited the car, he said, "Goodbye."

A few days later, we started arguing again. I told him I couldn't stand this relationship anymore. He was silent for a few minutes, then firmly said, "Okay," before he hung up.

I was so angry that I was shaking. A part of me didn't want to continue this for another second. I didn't even love him. The idea of being in love and belonging made me unable to let go of him.

I hung up, and a few days passed by.

Again, as I had done during the past few months, I got more anxious when I wasn't talking to him. I wondered what he was doing and why he hadn't called. Finally, I called him.

He answered the phone with a cold voice. After talking for a few seconds, he said, "I don't want to be back together again."

I had not expected to hear that, but I was too proud to ask him why or insist. So, I said, "Okay," and we both hung up.

I could feel he was serious, and maybe, deep down, I also wanted this relationship to end. However, I was naïve and needy. It was hard to realise that a girl like me had a lifetime ahead of her. All I could see was now. I was not familiar with the future.

The end of a relationship is not the end of the world. But I was not mature enough to understand many things. I didn't even know men. I had no idea about a right or wrong relationship. There was no education in our schools or society for a teenage girl. We were even banned from spending time with boys. So, how could we learn about them and have proper, meaningful relationships in the future?

How a woman is expected to get married and grow into a relationship when she is still learning about herself at that age is beyond comprehension. Society banned everything, and we were under much pressure outside the home.

There was much talking inside my home to guide me in the right direction, but I wasn't close to my mom and couldn't talk to her about my relationship with Abtin. I wasn't close to my dad, either. Being afraid of him, I certainly couldn't open up to him.

At the time, my emotions were so high and out of control that no one could enter the world that I was living in. And it was not a happy one. I had to face the reality that this relationship was not going anywhere.

The reality was harsh and unkind. There was no mercy, no compassion, not even someone who could explain the answers to my questions. I was in my little, lonely world, out of a relationship after three years, alone without any motivation to look forward to the future, and dealing with the rest of the world, which I wasn't really keen about. That was my reality. That's exactly how I felt.

## *Flashback*

The week after this happened, I went north with Ana and Maryam and stayed at a friend's villa for a few days. On the way back, we had that terrible accident that I luckily survaived.

# PART V
New Beginnings

# CHAPTER 15

## Meeting New Friends

### *The Party After the Hospital*

After my accident and being hospitalized for a few days, my mom dropped me off at Maryam and Ana's house. I was feeling light and rested. Maybe it was the effects of drugs that were still in my body. I was numb and emotionless, too.

The feeling of not being with Abtin did not bother me anymore. It was nice to spend time with Maryam and Ana and not be alone at home. I didn't want to face my dad, either.

We were invited to a friend's house for a small party. Their house was a beautiful villa away from Tehran with a big pool and massive yard.

When we arrived, we parked in a parking garage inside the grounds and went in. There were a few people, including our host, Salar, a friend of our friend, who was a cool, good-looking guy we had met before when we'd been skiing.

I started to feel a little bored, but I was okay. Maryam was dating a guy who was also there. We had a drink and chatted. The music was on low because we were talking. Salar, our host, invited us to sit outside, so we all went onto the balcony and sat around a table.

It was almost midnight when Maryam whispered, "Oh well, at least we got to the house. I know there's no party, and you guys got a little bored, but it isn't too bad." She was trying to convince us that driving one hour to get there had been worth it instead of staying at home.

Ana and I looked at each other with a questionable look, and then I said, "Yes, it's actually nice to be here."

On the other side of the table, Salar suddenly said, "Some friends are coming soon."

We looked at him, wondering who he meant. While we were talking, the doorbell rang. "They have arrived," Salar said.

We were quite surprised and looked at each other, trying to understand what was happening.

The big front yard door opened, and about five or six cars drove in. Their music was rather loud as they entered the parking area. The people who got out of the car looked energetic and happy. Some of them were wearing sunglasses, which looked quite strange at night. They came into the villa. We were so surprised seeing all of this, as if all of a sudden, the house had turned into a discotheque. Everyone was excited and talking loudly.

I was still digesting what was happening because we had been about to leave a minute before that. A couple of the new guests pulled a massive speaker out of their car and brought it inside. They plugged it in, and the music went through the roof. Maryam, Ana, and I were shocked by all this happening in just a few minutes.

Everyone entered the house, and suddenly, the small outdoor gathering had become a big, crazy party.

### Do you want to try one?

Salar pointed at me from the other side of the living room and asked me to come over.

When I arrived, he asked, "Do you want to take X?"

It was the first time that I had heard this, so I asked, "What's X?" I thought he was asking if I wanted to have Dex, which was a strong cough syrup and was known to make you high if you downed the whole bottle at once.

I was about to politely say, no, thank you. We had tried Dex once before when we were in the north, and it had made me so sick that I threw up everything within a few seconds. It was such a horrible experience that the smell stuck with me for some time.

But before I could say anything else, Salar said, "It's X—Ecstasy. Haven't you tried it before?" His tone made it clear that he was wondering how I didn't know about it.

"I haven't," I told him.

He showed me a blue pill, broke it into two halves, and gave me one. "Will it kill me?" I asked hesitantly.

He laughed. "No. Don't worry; you'll be okay."

I trusted him and swallowed the pill with some Coca-Cola. I said thanks, smiled and returned to sit on the couch next to a few other girls.

The new people who had arrived at the party were dancing. Sitting on the couch, I looked at their faces to see if I recognized anyone through their sunglasses which was also weird that they were wearing at night.

After a few minutes, I saw a tall guy who looked kind of familiar. I turned back to Mania, a girl sitting next to me, and asked her, pointing to him, "Do you know that guy? What is his name?"

She looked to where I was pointing. "I don't think so."

Right at that moment, he looked toward me and came my way. He leaned forward and asked, "Would you like to dance?" It all happened so quickly as I got up and danced with him.

As we danced, I started feeling something happening in my body. Of course, it was the effects of the Ecstasy.

We danced for a long time. I don't remember what we talked about, we did talk a lot too. Then he said he wanted to go out and get some fresh air. We went outside, sat in one of the open cars, and kissed. We exchanged numbers before we left that night.

A few days later, he called. He was Roozbeh, the guy I had met in the kitchen of our friend's house when I was still in a relationship with Abtin. He was charming, handsome, tall, and incredibly smart. He had studied mechanical engineering and was running a small packaging business. I was highly attracted to him, and meeting him made me completely forget about Abtin and our breakup.

He invited me to his house the next week. He lived alone in a two-bedroom apartment on the eastern side of town. His father had passed away a few years before. His only brother lived abroad.

He was athletic and worked out a lot. He also played the drums and electric guitar and asked me to listen to him play.

We talked a lot about different subjects. He talked fast. It was interesting to talk to him, and the fact that he jumped from subject to subject kept me excited and made me want to listen and follow up. He sounded like me—talking fast and trying to cover many areas simultaneously. I always felt I confused many people because I tended to change the subject suddenly and unknowingly, my brain always jumping in different directions.

It was fun to see someone who was the same. He could follow me, as well. Plus, everything we talked about interested me. It wasn't about shallow, unimportant subjects that many young people our age were interested in. It was about life, the future, improving, and many more meaningful subjects.

The next time we met was when he invited me to his friend's birthday party. That evening, I went to his house, and then his friend picked us up from there, and we drove to the party. It was full of people, and it was fun. We talked to other people, and he didn't feel the need to always stand next to me. I socialized, too with his friends and we had a good time.

Then, a week later, he said he was leaving with a couple of his friends on a bike trip. They were going to the mountains in northwestern Iran, and he wouldn't be back for a couple of weeks. We never talked about anything else.

When he was away, I often thought of him as I waited for him to return. I imagined when he would call me and tried to imagine what would happen next. I was a lot more mature than before and, I guess, less needy. This time, all I wanted was to know him and for us to spend more time together. I didn't care about the relationship as such.

He had told me that his birthday was close. But two weeks went by, and I didn't hear from him.

It was his birthday the week that I called him. He was back from the trip and picked up the phone. He wasn't as warm as the last time we'd spoken, so I didn't call him during the next three weeks. He didn't call me, either. I couldn't stop thinking about him, though.

The drama of my relationship with Abtin disappeared after meeting this guy. I had met a different group of people who could have fun despite everything that was banned in society. They could listen to loud music and dance. That was amazing. I was twenty years old, and it was the first time I could forget all the problems at university, home, and away from home and enjoy myself.

## *The Power of Connection*

So, taking Ecstasy, listening to music, and dancing seemed to be the answer and the key to my new world. The people who partied like that seemed so cool and careless, and they were extremely different from those I'd known before. They were people who understood different things.

I talked about it with Maryam many times, arguing about how, if someone hadn't taken Ecstasy, he or she was not able to see many things and how those people are backward and stupid. Maryam had tried Ecstasy sometime after that party for the first time, too.

In our young, inexperienced world, Ecstasy was now so much more important than everything else. We were all fascinated by the mysterious world we had discovered in the society we lived in until that time.

It was the beginning of summer, and we were often invited to these parties, many of which were held in the mountains, a one-hour drive outside of Tehran, where the Shamshak Ski Resort was. There were a lot of villas and apartments around the ski resort.

At home, things had changed. My dad was not as strict as before. I guess that he and Mom had concluded that they should give me some freedom. But they were watching me closely. By then, I had run away from home a few times to my grandparents' house, my friend's house, the north, and Maryam's parents. Of course, I had come back home every time.

My accident was a turning point. Deep down, I knew my accident made people realize how much pain I was going through. The main point was probably focused on my parents and not Abtin because, after all, he was out of my life and thoughts. It was my parents who became more understanding and more friendly.

This comment is not intended to encourage others to copy my stupid actions. It is to illustrate the whole reason behind what happened. It is to show compassion for girls in my situation and tell them they are not alone. They will find their way without having to go through this traumatic experiences.

Parents need to understand their children's emotions and realize that, at this age, rationality is not dominant. Their emotions are often so high and intense that they sometimes cannot see the right direction, no matter how much you talk to them and try to convince them. Being friends with them will rescue them from being drawn to the wrong people and environment.

So, that's how the party scene took another level for me, and a different chapter started.

Meeting Roozbeh also showed me that the world was not as limited as Abtin and his friends' worlds. Getting drunk, playing musical instruments, and singing is not all there is to life. He is not the only person in the world. There are more interesting, attractive, and much nicer, smarter guys to meet.

## A New Chapter

After Roozbeh returned from his bike trip in the mountains, and two weeks after, when we didn't talk, I met him again at his house. Our meet ups happened more and more, we never talked about our relationship. It seemed as if he wanted to keep the relationship between us. I didn't mind that. I liked him a lot and enjoyed the time we spent together.

Not having him also fed my desperate need to be in love with someone. I spent a lot of time thinking about him and looking forward to seeing him. Spending time with him helped me completely forget about my relationship with Abtin. My mind was occupied with it even at parties, and I wasn't attracted to anyone else.

I certainly had more freedom at home. My parents bought me a black Nissan Patrol. I loved it. It was my dream car at the time, even though it consumed a lot of gas, and I had to fill up the tank once a week. I think something wasn't right with the engine. I was even allowed to spend nights away. These nights away were mostly in Shemshak, although a lot of the time, I would get back to Tehran and stay at Roozbeh place, of course without my parents knowing.

He would also call me every few days to meet up. We would go to his apartment, and he would play his drums, and we would listen to the Red Hot Chili Peppers, smoke, and talk. The parties, on the other hand, were crazy. The music, the DJs, the young people like us, all taking Ecstasy and dancing under flashing blue lights to the sound of music resonating from loudspeakers. There was always the scare of getting arrested by the local committee.

We never planned to go to those parties together. I saw Roozbeh in the crowd several times, but he always seemed busy hanging out with his friends. I didn't understand him well. We were all in separate groups, so we didn't have to encounter or face each other.

Still, I wasn't satisfied with it. It wasn't what I was looking for. I didn't want to have a hidden relationship, yet that's what it seemed Roozbeh wanted.

I tried to tell him how I felt a couple of times, but I was vague about it. Regardless, he tried to call me more after I had tried to express myself, and he seemed to be trying.

Of course, I wasn't doing anything more. I was inexperienced and didn't know how to handle things, what to ask, or even what I wanted. So, the relationship kept on going at the same pace as before. We still saw each other almost every week, sometimes more.

In the fall, two friends and I rented an apartment from villagers in Shemshak at the top of the mountains and spent most weekends there. My parents knew this, but my dad barely talked to me about it.

It felt something was missing from these meetings with Roozbeh. I wasn't happy with how we just met; we were intimate and then talked a couple of times until we met again. I didn't like not hanging out with his friends and not being officially in a relationship.

## A Common Dream

One day, Roozbeh told me he needed to see an eye doctor, and I offered to give him a ride. The doctor's office was on a busy street, so I told him I'd drive around until he was done, then will take him back. On the way back, we talked about leaving Iran. We talked about it all the way back towards his home and he told me that he liked the idea, too.

It felt like we both dreamed of a day when we could live in a better place, which was a nice feeling. We talked about this often after that.

# CHAPTER 16

## I am a Different Person Now

### *Abtin Returns For an Apology*

Abtin had left for Dubai and had started working there. He came back to visit in January of the next year. He called me and asked if I wanted to meet up. I told him I was out of town, in Shemshak, and would be back on that Friday. I didn't mind seeing him. My feelings were completely neutral toward him, and I wasn't feeling any emotions. It was as if I hadn't ever known him and nothing had happened between us. That was strange to me, but I was so relieved that I felt that way. He didn't matter in my life anymore and couldn't hurt me.

That weekend, my friends and I were invited to a big party in a villa close to our rented place. We all headed there, and, of course, everybody we knew in town was there. A few of roozbeh's friends were there, too. I was hoping to see him, but he didn't show up.

The music was loud. Many people were dancing, and some were talking. We were there for a few hours when Ana approached me in the middle of the party.

"Abtin is here," she told me.

I was a different person after what I had gone through. I was in love with a new person, even though we met once or twice a week at his place, and he was not emotionally available.

Somehow, I was being sensible, but I felt numb, too. It was like I was awake in another world. This world was more enjoyable, and there seemed to be less harm in it.

I couldn't believe Abtin had come all the way up to the village in the mountains, and I was angry that he hadn't even told me that he was coming and had just shown up.

I told Maryam and Ana that I was going, and I left. Abtin drove up the mountains with the same white beat-up truck and followed my car to the villa.

We went back to our place that we had rented, which was always really cold. I made some tea and asked him coldly, "Why didn't you tell me you were coming?"

"I wanted to see you," he answered.

Deep down, I started to experience a feeling of anger mixed with bittersweet revenge. I replied, "Oh, well, you are welcome to stay here till the morning if you like."

"Haven't you missed me?" he asked.

It was funny and disturbing how he would dare ask me something like that, knowing all I had gone through!

We talked briefly, and I told him, "Listen, you made me not want to live anymore. With what you did to me, how can you even have the courage to think I have any feelings left for you?"

We barely slept and kept talking. Mostly, he explained why the relationship hadn't been working and had to end. He also tried to explain how he wanted us to be together again now that he was back. I tried to tell him I had no feelings for him anymore.

I was so hurt that I didn't want to be friends or see him again. I told him I had completely moved on from that relationship and was now living in a different world and mixing in a different crowd. He told me that I shouldn't hang out with those people and that attending those parties was not in keeping with my family's class.

However his group of friends seemed so boring to me. And being his girlfriend also seemed to be such a stupid thing.

I was so calm that every word coming out of my mouth was brutal. It was almost close to dawn, and I could see his eyes were teary and looking desperate. But I didn't care about him. I was happy that I had told him everything I wanted to say, and I was happy that I had no emotion.

We left the place together quietly so we wouldn't wake Ana, Maryam, and our other friends, who were all sleeping. It was around nine a.m. It was cold and snowing outside.

When we came out, I saw a big guy standing right outside our chalet, wearing a unique, black, woollen Russian hat. He said, "Hi, Sarah, I am Parsa. We are your new neighbors." Renting the apartment next door.

# PART VI

Another Man in My Life

# CHAPTER 17

# Start of an Obsessive Relationship

### *Introduction to Parsa*

I recognized him. He was the son of my English teacher, Ms. Lia who was from England. I had attended her private English classes since I was ten years old. They held great Christmas parties with a lot of fun activities for kids back then at their house.

I had met him when we were younger. He was a tall, good looking guy. He and his beautiful sister, Sheri, spoke English with British accents.

Having barely slept after talking to Abtin all night, I looked up, saw him with his funny Russian hat, and said, "Hi." Abtin, who was pissed off about everything we had talked about throughout the night before, said, "Hi," quickly as he walked past.

I told Parsa that my car had gotten stuck on the way up last night, and we had to leave it in the middle of the road. "You did the right thing," Parsa said. "It's not safe to bring it up at all—it's too icy."

"I remember you from your mom's classes," I told him, and then we chatted for a few minutes before I left.

The rear lights were broken when Abtin and I got to the car. It seemed as if someone had tried to come up, then slipped down backwards and hit my car from the front. I wasn't happy to see this, so I looked at Abtin. In my mind, I blamed him because he had gate-crashed my party, kept me talking all night, and left my car in the middle of the road.

We were lucky it had not slipped down the valley, as the road was incredibly steep and icy.

"Can you fix the lights?" I asked.

"I'll get them for you and replace them," he agreed.

Then we drove my car down to the main road. Abtin got out, and we said goodbye. He had an upset face but showed no emotion as he left.

I felt a sense of relief. It was as if all night had been so intense that I just wanted him not to be there and to leave me alone. I was even surprised about my own feelings and how things had changed in such a short time. I just didn't want him to be around.

Wow! What happened to all that love that I had felt? I matured from those first love-related emotions that were life or death. Now, I knew that it wasn't the case. You won't die when you break up with someone. Seeing him with that desperate face and behaving in a way opposite to how he used to behave was another experience, too.

So, men can be desperate and emotional, too! Wow! That was interesting, as well, to me, as I was a girl who didn't know much about men.

## Valentine's Party and the Start of a New Relationship

Soon, Parsa and I started talking on the phone. The first time I spoke with him, I had just returned home from dinner with all the girls. Maryam and Ana pushed me to call him, and I put the speaker on while we all listened in the car. I told him that we were all in the car, and he said hello to everyone. Then we talked and joked around.

After this, I was still hesitant to call him again, and I wasn't sure if it was me or Ana that he was interested in. But my friends assured me that I was wrong; he was clearly into me and that I should call him back.

So, the next day, I called. He invited me to dinner, and we went on our first date. It was a nice, casual evening, and I felt he was a nice human being who was respectful toward me. This was quite the opposite of my previous relationships. I really liked it. He was charming, good-looking, and looked really into me.

A week after that first dinner, we were invited to a mutual friend's birthday on Valentine's Day. Once again, it was at Shemshak Ski Resort, in a twelfth-floor condo. Parsa said he could pick me up.

I was excited about going where all my friends were, with Parsa as my new date. He picked me up in his old green Land Rover, and we headed to Arvin's birthday party.

It was a big party, and almost everyone I knew was there. The music was loud, and many were dancing. People looked at us curiously, seeing us together and joking around with us, asking if we were dating. After the relationship with Abtin, it was the first time I was being seen with someone within our circle of friends, and it was exciting.

I definitely liked him, it was differed from how I had liked Abtin. I wasn't needy; I just liked him. We had so much fun at the party that night. He was attractive, popular, and definitely a gentleman. He was so different from Abtin. He treated me with respect, and I appreciated that a lot.

After the party, it was official that we were girlfriend and boyfriend. The small studio apartment that he lived in was attached to a bigger house where his parents lived. It was a short drive from our house, only a few minutes.

He worked at the family's European-style boutique that sold British-brand clothes in the shopping mall across the street from our house. They stocked a variety of nice brand-name clothes, mostly men's, that his dad imported from England. Parsa, his mom, and his dad ran the shop.

His dad was strict with him and always checked on him, ensuring he was at work at the right time, clocked in and out and worked properly.

His dad had been a flight attendant who had fallen in love with his mom, a beautiful English lady, and they had married. They lived in Tehran, also spent a lot of time in London.

His sister lived in London with her husband, and they sometimes came to visit. She had been diagnosed with cancer a few years before, which had resulted in the family going through a difficult time. But she survived the illness.

# CHAPTER 18

## Traveling with Parsa

### *Planning a Visit to Parsa's Parents' Villa*

Almost one month after that, around mid-March, it was the Iranian New Year. We decided to go north and stay at Parsa's parents' villa. We invited a few of our friends, too. I had talked to Roozbeh a few times and told him I was in a relationship with Parsa but had not seen him.

He joked around, asking, "Are you in love?" "Yes, maybe," I answered.

He respected what I said and didn't call me to meet up like before, he kept in touch.

Parsa and I were excited about the trip to the north. There were always two weeks of holidays starting a day or two before the New Year and continuing for thirteen days afterwards. People usually celebrated, travelled, and visited each other during this time.

I planned to drive my car north so they didn't stop us on the road for not being related and driving in the same car together.

I needed to check to see if the car was in good enough condition. Parsa suggested that I take it to a repair shop that he knew. So, I took my car to the shop, and a mechanic started working on the car.

I called Parsa from the phone inside the store and told him I was there. We woud let each other know where we were during the day, whether at home or work, etc.

It took some time for the guy to check the car and fix a few minor things. When he was done, I left and went home. I called Parsa from there.

We were extremely excited about the trip and counting the minutes until we were leaving just before the New Year.

After talking for a few minutes, he told me what he had done that day, and I told him about the repair shop and that I had to wait a few hours. Then I realized from his words that he had called the repair shop and asked the guy. He knew exactly when I had gotten there and what time I had left. He checked on me to see if I was lying or told the truth.

I was surprised and turned off at the same time that he was so suspicious. I had told him the truth and didn't have a reason to lie. We were only a month into our relationship, and he didn't even believe me? Wow! That was too much. I still liked him a lot, but somehow, that had changed my perception of his character. Nevertheless, I didn't mention anything.

## *Trip to the North without Permission from Parents*

I was in the last year of university and going to graduate with a Bachelor of Arts in English Language Translation.

Things at home had changed, but I still could not freely ask to go on a trip with my boyfriend. I knew my mom had already told my dad everything about Parsa, he never acknowledged his name or acknowledged his existence.

I had to lie and say that I was going on the trip north with Maryam's family and not with my friends and boyfriend, as the word *boyfriend* had no meaning in his dictionary.

Finally, the date that we were leaving town came. I was so excited. I had travelled with Abtin and a few of our friends once before, but this was only the second time.

I had changed so much since that time. I was much more confident in this relationship and enjoyed my time with Parsa. We talked a lot and had many mutual interests.

We also went to his parents' villa in the north with many friends who were staying there with us. For us, it was a rare opportunity to be together. Maryam and Ana were coming, too, to stay a few days with us, then spend a few days at the villa of one of our friends close by.

We got on the road, girls in one car and boys in another, following each other. Some other friends were going to join us there.

Though I liked Parsa quite a lot, I was doubting his personality and the fact that he had checked up on me about something so silly. Still, I didn't let that get to me and planned to enjoy the trip as much as possible.

That year, the Iranian New Year holidays were at the same time as the holy month of Moharram, the holy Islamic day when people would mourn. The Islamic belief is that the second Imam gets wounded with a poisonous sword in a battle defending Islam and dies a day later. The day he got wounded is called Tasooa, and the day he passed away is called Ashoora. They are important religious events in Iran.

The Arabic calendar, which also reflects the Islamic religious days, is based on lunar rotation and is different from the Iranian calendar, which is based on solar rotation and changes on the first day of spring on March 21st. It has been this way since the time of the Zoroastrians who ruled Persia before the Arab Muslim conquest and the rise of Islam in Iran.

On our calendars, we have two dates: the main Iranian calendar date based on solar rotation and the Arabic date shown as small numbers on the corners to remind us what religious or holy day it is.

We were aware that these days were mourning days. It was forbidden to have parties or celebrations of any sort. We were trying to take all possible precautions to ensure that we wouldn't be stopped by the committee at checkpoints on the road so that we would get to our destination without any trouble.

We turned the music a little louder in my car and joked around, singing along with the songs and talking about our plans for the trip. Other cars, including a girl's car and Parsa and another boy's car, were following us, so we were escorted on the road. We only stopped at two places to use restrooms and didn't risk stopping at any restaurants, rather heading straight to the villa. Their place was located in an area in the northern belt where the mountains and sea meet each other and are at the closest point to one another. Driving on the road, you have a deep, green mountain on one side and the beautiful Caspian Sea on the other side. I think it's one of the most beautiful scenary of the northern part of Iran.

Their villa wasn't big. It had two bedrooms, one bathroom, and a living room with a cute fireplace. Everything was neat and clean.

We brought all the food from Tehran inside and placed it in the kitchen or fridge. We were going to barbeque that night. Then we rested for a while before we went for a long walk in the hills around the neighbourhood.

I loved Shomal (the north) and the smell of fresh rice mixed with the ocean breeze, which had many different scents. I also loved nature and getting away from Tehran and all its troubles. Shomal was like heaven, and I could forget about everything there and be the person I wanted to be when I was there.

When we returned from our walk, the boys started preparing the barbecue. We helped them by cooking the rice and preparing the dishes for dinner.

We had brought two big speakers with us, and after our late lunch, which was also an early dinner, we partied throughout the night and then went to sleep when it was nearly morning. The next day, everybody slept until noon.

After Parsa had made a nice breakfast, we all headed to our friend's Roozbeh villa, which was close by. Their large villa was located up on the hill with big windows on both sides, so sitting in their living room, you could see the green belt and the sea from far and above. It was dreamy. He said some people could stay there, as there was more space. We stayed until later that night and then returned to our place.

Everything was so nice, absolutely wonderful. Parsa and I were really into each other. We loved to walk and would talk for hours. It was great that we could spend so much time together without worrying about anything.

# CHAPTER 19
## The Horrors of Arrest

### *The decision to go to Arvin's Party*

The next day, some more friends joined us. We were happy to see them, and they told us about a party held by Arvin, an old friend of ours who was staying in his parents' villa a couple of hours' drive away from where we were.

Arvin was the same friend who had his birthday party in his apartment in the Shemshak Ski Resort area on Valentine's Day, when Parsa and I had gone out together for the first time. We were both close to him, and everyone really liked him. He was a kind, cool guy. Our mutual friends told us that he had invited everyone to his villa near Khezershahr resort.

Everyone started debating whether to go or not. Parsa called him, and Arvin insisted we should go so we wouldn't miss out he said "it's going to be a great party."

I wasn't a fan of going there, partly because we had to drive for two hours. I was also scared of going to a big party. I was worried that if anything happened, I wouldn't know what I should do or even how I could tell my dad.

After a long discussion, with everybody giving their opinion, we finally decided to go. Some friends were excited to go and meet new people. They weren't couples and were getting a bored staying in our place.

Late that afternoon, everyone started getting ready for the party. We left the villa early in the evening and were still cautious, though it was usually less strict once you were in the north rather than on the road from Tehran. I left my car at the villa.

We talked on the road, listened to music, and were totally ignorant that the two Islamic holy days were starting the next day. In our world, all that mattered was having fun and finding an opportunity to compensate for our lack of social freedom as young adults. In effect, parties like this were the same as going to a nightclub, which we didn't have in our country.

When we arrived, many cars were parked outside, mostly close to the main road. You could see all the cars gathered in one place. We could hear music that wasn't too loud but could still be heard. We were excited when we parked, but we didn't consider that all these cars would attract the attention of anyone who went past, including the committee and local people.

When we walked in, the music was so loud, and the villa was full of people. They had covered all the windows with fibre sheets and blankets to avoid letting the sound get out too much. Salar, the same guy who had given me ecstasy the first time, was playing tempo.

Arvin welcomed us warmly and showed us where the drinks were. The bar was full of cold beers and different kinds of alcohol. I knew some people in the crowd but hadn't met others before. Everyone scattered into the crowd to talk to people they knew and hang out with their friends.

Parsa got us drinks, and he gave me a small piece of an ecstasy pill while we were dancing in the crowd, chatting to our friends. I couldn't see any of our friends we had come with, not even Maryam or Ana. Musice was load and there were many people.

I told Parsa that I was going to the toilet and headed there. When I came back, I saw him talking closely to two girls. Of course, because of the loud music, there was no other way that they could hear each other without huddling together.

I knew one of the girls and didn't like her at all. I had seen her a few times before.

When she saw me, she reached out to hug me with one arm and the other to hug Parsa. She said in English, "Oh my God, you two are such a cute couple!"

Parsa answered, "Thank you," in English.

I looked coldly at Parsa, and a few minutes later, the girls left and went to the other side of the room.

## Getting Arrested and Going to Jail

When we were alone again, I told him I didn't like that girl, Elnaz. I wanted to know why she was so friendly and talking so close to him. We started arguing.

"She's always like that. What can you do about it? It's not like you can control her," he said.

While talking, we heard someone banging loudly on the door as if using their fist. Someone quickly turned down the music, and then we heard someone say, "The committee. Open the door, or we will break it down!"

Even though we were used to dealing with situations like this, we were all scared. Usually, the host of a party, or someone who could talk to the committee firmly, would step out and give them some money and chat with them to convince them that we would stop. That worked most of the time, although they sometimes had to pay *a lot* of money.

This was not the same. They didn't give anyone a chance to explain or pay a bribe. They just continued to bang loudly on the door to get in.

Parsa pulled me quickly toward the top floor, where a room was under the attic. He said, "Follow me. We can jump from the roof to the neighbour's house."

I followed Parsa to the attic. There were already a few people there, trying to jump onto the neighbour's roof so that they could run away from the back.

From the top of the roof, I saw a religious Molla standing in the front yard, and I got even more scared. I had never seen a Molla go to parties and be on the committee arresting people. What was he doing there?

Then, a big, tall guy who was trying to get into the house shouted angrily, "Haj agha," which is the prefix used for religious masters, "They won't open the door."

The Molla replied, "Break down the door."

This was so scary. I told Parsa, "Jump," but he didn't. "Why won't you jump?"

"I can't. I am heavy, and the roof will go down," he said.

Some people ran from behind, but we were stuck on the roof. Even though I was scared of jumping down, I would have, but Parsa held me back. Within a few minutes, the same big guy who had been shouting to get into the house came up to the roof and pulled us all back down into the house.

They separated the girls from the boys and told us, "Head down to the outside of the house, in the street where a few pickup trucks are parked."

My heart was pounding. I couldn't feel anything. I was numb, probably from the effect of the ecstasy pills that we had taken before the committee had arrived. The only thing I could think of was to run away.

I couldn't imagine my dad hearing that I had been arrested in the north and being told he had to come and get me Out of jail. The thought of it made me nauseous. I had to find a way to get away.

The big guy shouted as he was leading us toward the cars, "They are all naked."

For a second, I couldn't believe what I was hearing. Were we really naked? Then I understood what he meant. We were not wearing hijabs, and that, to him, meant we were naked.

The two girls in front of me ran toward the back of the house, and I ran after them. The big guy followed us. He took out his gun and started shooting into the air. I couldn't believe that he actually did that.

I tried to hide on the side of the wall as I ran toward the back of the house with the other two girls. It was dark, but there wasn't much distance between me and the big guy. He saw me and grabbed the back of my T-shirt, pushing me toward the alley that led to the front of the house where their trucks were. He told me in an angry voice, "Move!"

I walked with him. I was scared but determined to find a way to get out.

As we arrived at the pickup truck, I saw all the girls sitting in the back, and everyone was really upset and quiet. I looked at Maryam, and I guessed she knew what was happening in my mind. She knew me better than anyone else. She knew my tolerance and patience to go through something like this was low. She also knew how scared I would be to even think about my dad finding out what had happened and having to come and get me out of jail.

I started pretending to have heart pain. Within a few minutes, the driver came to take us to the police station. The house was surrounded by the committee's pickup trucks, and soldiers were everywhere.

## Overnight Prison in The North

When we got to the police station, they told us to get off the truck and head into the station to a small room close to the entrance where the head office was located.

"I have heart pain," I told the guy who was leading us toward the room, pretending that I wasn't feeling good. "Can I have some water?"

He believed me and came back with a bottle of water.

I continued to pretend I was sick. Even the other people who caught up with me, including my friends, believed I wasn't feeling good, and they looked worried.

One of the girls who was taller that all of us and I had met a few times, stood up and angrily told the guy who had brought me water, "She doesn't feel good. She has heart pain."

The guy responded rudely, "Shut up and sit back in your chair."

The girl got angry and threw the bottle of water at him.

I didn't want anyone else to get involved, but she was defending me and was worried that something might happen to me. She was upset and angry.

Everyone was really unhappy. They whispered, "Oh my God, what are they going to do?" or, "When my parents find out, they won't be happy."

I felt all these things, but my fear was beyond thinking about them. I was determined that I didn't want to be in this situation and knew I had to do something about it.

Now that we were inside the police station, the only solution was to pretend that I wasn't feeling good, so I kept telling the soldiers who were checking on us. I also lay on the floor and pretended not to be able to breathe. I hoped I could let my friends and the girl defending me know that, by doing this, I was trying to find a way to escape and its not real so they don't get worried for me, but it was impossible.

I was actually not feeling well at all. I was extremely scared and was in a panic, imagining and thinking how my father would react when he found out and how upset my mom would be to have to deal with all of this.

We had been arrested after midnight, and I remember that when we were at the police station, it was around 1:30 to two a.m. Some time had passed, I wasn't sure what the time was when one of the committee members came in and told everyone to get up and head down to the basement's temporary jail. He told me to go to the office of the head of the station. Everyone was so upset and scared as they all headed downstairs.

I walked alone toward the office, which was located near the entrance at the front of the station.

The assistant to the head of the station, who was a man of about sixty years, was sitting there. He had blue eyes and fair features.

"Okay, so I've heard that you are not feeling well," he said sarcastically while writing some notes on a paper.

"Yes, sir," I replied. "I have heart pain. I need to get the pills I take for my heart problem."

I felt I got his attention a little more as he asked, "Where are your pills?"

"I left them at the villa. I need to take them," I responded in a serious tone.

The deputy looked at the other man talking to me and said, "Take her back to the villa to find her pills."

### *Back to the Villa*

I felt there was some hope because they believed me, but I was so scared and traumatized that I could barely feel anything. They told me to follow them to the entrance and get into the pickup truck, one of the same ones that had brought us in. We headed toward the villa where the party had been held a few hours before.

The driver and the other guy in the car seemed a little less aggressive and started talking to me, asking, "Why do you do things like going to parties that are banned?"

I replied in a sorry, low tone, "I swear I didn't want to go at all. My friends took me. They pushed me to go with them and said it was all going to be fun. If my father finds out, it's going to be really bad. My dad is your colleague, too. He is a court official."

My dad was a licensed inspector in his own field. "agronomy". So, when there were disputes and conflicts, the court would call him to judge agriculture-related cases, etc. He had told me a few times that this was important. He was licensed by the government and worked on a case for one of his friends who owned a nursery near Tehran.

"He is a licensed inspector and would never let me go to places like this. I am really ashamed of what I have done. I don't know how I will ever be able to look him in the eyes if he finds out."

I arrived at the villa with the driver and the other guy who had accompanied us. The house was still surrounded by soldiers. They were everywhere. I saw two of them on the roof, as well. They were also at the back of the house.

We headed inside, where they searched the house, moving cans of beer and liquor bottles.

I looked at the ground. In some places, there were ecstasy pills that had been trodden on and smashed. It looked like white powder on the floor inside the house. I guessed some of the other kids had done that while they were arresting us.

The driver told me to look for my heart pills quickly. I found my bag in the room that I had left behind. When they were arresting us, Parsa had given me the ecstasy pills and a 50,000 Iranian Tooman money note, so that I would at least have some money on me. I quickly took the pills out of my bag, threw them under the bed, and got out of the room with my bag.

I told them that I had found my bag, but I couldn't find my heart pills. The driver and the other guy said, "Okay, but we can't wait here anymore. We should head back to the station quickly."

I hoped for a chance to run from there, but there was no way with all those soldiers inside and around the house. We got back into the pickup truck. They sat in the front, and I sat in the back as we headed back to the police station.

## *Pleading to be Released*

"Can you please help me and tell them to let me go? Please, I swear I won't do this ever again," I said, trying anything I could, hoping they might feel sorry for me and let me go.

They didn't say anything.

When we arrived at the station, the judge, wearing a customary religious dress, was waiting for the drivers to take him home. I was getting out of the truck as he came to sit inside.

The driver told him, "Haj agha, this girl is innocent. They misled her and forced her to go to the party. Her dad is a licensed court inspector. Is there any way that you can let her go?"

I didn't hear what he replied, but I guessed he told them to talk to the deputy assistant, the same old man with blue eyes and fair skin who was in charge. Then he left with the driver to go to his house, and the other guy told me to return to the station.

We went inside to the assistant of the head of the station's office, who asked what had happened. "Did you find your heart pills?"

"No, sir, I did not," I replied.

The other guy, who had taken me back to the villa, said, "Haj agha, the religious judge, asked if you could let her go. She is innocent. She didn't want to go to this party. They forced her to go."

He shook his head as if he couldn't do anything, and tears started dripping off my face again.

A few hours had passed since we had arrived. He didn't want to let me go. *Oh my God, what should I do?* I started acting again.

"My heart is in pain, sir. I have heart issues. Please, let me go."

"What kind of issues do you have? You seemed to be fine a few minutes ago," he replied sarcastically.

They had taken all my friends downstairs to another room. It was only us. A soldier was now positioned in the cabin outside the station as a security guard. The driver and the other guy kept coming in and out of the room. It seemed as if one of them was trying to convince the deputy to let me go, but he was enjoying this and had a smile and a friendly tone while talking to me and asking questions.

A few minutes passed. I wasn't losing hope. I had come so far. They should let me go. I kept on pretending and saying my heart was in pain, begging them to please do something. "It's serious. I need to take them."

The deputy beckoned to one of the drivers. They chatted, and the driver told me, "Let's go."

"Where are we going?"

"To the hospital so a doctor can check you," he replied.

We went to his truck with the other guy accompanying us and headed toward the hospital only a few minutes from the station. I hoped the doctor would help me, so I took out the 50,000 Tooman note that Parsa had given me, hiding it with my fist clenched.

They sent me to an examination room. A doctor with a black beard and a serious face asked in his northern accent, "What is going on with you?"

I didn't like his tone, and I felt even more nervous as he entered the room. There was no compassion you usually hear in a doctor's voice. It felt like he was disgusted or angry with me.

"It's my heart. I have to have my heart pills because I have heart issues," I replied.

He looked at me as he filled up a syringe. He told me to turn my back and then injected me with something. Then he said sarcastically, "So, you have issues, right?"

With the money, I begged, "Please, let me stay here. I have been misled. My parents will come and get me soon." Then I showed him the money note.

He still had a cloth with alcohol in his hand. He squeezed it out onto my face, above my eyes, while I was still lying on the bed. Then he swore, using bad words, and said, "Nothing is wrong with you. Get the hell out of here."

I screamed from the pain of the alcohol in my eyes and couldn't believe that he had actually done that. I was so scared that I jumped off the bed and ran toward the door where the driver and his friend were waiting.

I don't know what happened during the next few minutes. My eyes were burning from the alcohol that he had squeezed over my face. I was scared and disappointed.

We went back to the police station again. I could feel it was early morning, although it was still dark.

We arrived, and I again sat in the front room where the deputy's desk was. I was tired but still had not given up. I was thinking so fast, but as much as I thought, I couldn't come up with a solution or the next plan.

Half an hour passed, and I saw a lady enter the station. She was concerned, asking what had happened, looking around as if she was looking for someone. I realized she was one of the kid's mothers.

I didn't know her, but I heard her daughter's name and realized that she was one of the three girls whose friend kept talking to Parsa in English at the party and about whom we had argued. They were talking in the corridor, and I was in the room.

## Escape to Freedom

While I was trying to hear what she was saying to the blue-eyed man in charge, the driver came into the room and said, "Listen, you should leave asap."

I couldn't believe whether I had heard what he was trying to tell me correctly. I listened more carefully.

"If you stay, and the head of the station comes, there won't be any other way for you to get out."

I was shocked. He really was helping me run away. Then he said, "Quickly, get up and go."

I did, and he went toward the end of the corridor where the deputy and the mom were talking. The guy was trying to help me by distracting them. He asked them a question loudly while I snuck out of the room and exited the station. My heart was pounding so loudly that I could hear it in my throat. As I stepped out, the soldier acting as security asked,

"Hey, what about my treat?"

I stepped into his little cabin and said, "Please, lower your voice." Then I remembered the Tooman note and gave it to him. I didn't wait another second and started running as fast as possible.

I had never run so fast in my life. My heart was pounding loudly, and I was breathing in and out so fast. I ran along the main street of the town where the station was located, along the seafront. It was the only main street, and there were alleys off it. I got far enough from the station until

I couldn't see it anymore, and there were barely any people in the street. It was almos six a.m.

Some people were in a line, waiting to buy fresh bread. They were surprised to see me. I didn't have makeup on, wearing jeans and sneakers. I had my scarf and manteaux, a long cover-up to the knees, buttoned up in the front, but I could easily be recognized as a girl who wasn't from that area or as a Tehrani girl, as they used to say when I went to the school there during the war.

I realized it wasn't safe to run or walk in the streets anymore, so I headed toward the back streets, hoping to find a route parallel to the main road toward the other side of the town, away from the station. Then I could get a taxi and return to Parsa's parents' villa.

I didn't have a mobile phone, but Parsa did, and he gave it to me at the last minute in case I needed to call my parents. I suddenly heard it ring. I picked it up quickly while looking around me to ensure no one was nearby, watching.

It was one of my friends calling from inside the police station. I didn't recognize who it was, but I guessed it might be Ana. She said, "Sarah, hide wherever you are. They found out you escaped and have sent two pickup trucks to search for you." Then she hung up quickly.

It was early morning, and I was shivering. I looked toward the main street and saw a green pickup truck pass by. I was on the back street, but I was still scared that they would see me.

I stepped onto a small piece of land surrounded by brick walls. A small part of the brick wall was broken, so I could get in. Then I ran toward the other side and jumped over another wall, thinking I could find my way out of the town that way, avoiding the main street. However, as soon as I got over the second wall, I slipped in the mud and nearly hit a few chickens running around.

I was shocked to see them move around so fast and make such a noise. I stopped where I was as I realized that this might be someone's house.

The owner, a tall, big-boned lady who looked like a farmer, came outside. She saw me, and her eyes got wide and round. She kept staring at me without saying anything. We both froze for a few seconds and then I quickly jumped out of there and ran as fast as I could to escape her house. I was careful to keep away from the main street, too.

I didn't know how much time had passed, but I could feel I was almost on the other side of town. It had been more than half an hour since my friend called me from the police station.

I looked around carefully to make sure I didn't see any of their trucks and then headed to the main street, hoping I could find a taxi service.

It was almost seven a.m. The sun had come up, and more people were in the streets. I started walking normally on the pavement and saw a man approaching me. I asked, "Excuse me, do you know where I can find a taxi service around here?"

He looked at me curiously but answered without pause, "There is a taxi service shop farther down at the roundabout called Setare Taxi."

I couldn't stop at the side of the street and get a normal cab, so I had to get a private taxi to take me back to Parsa's parents' villa.

I thanked the man and started walking faster toward the roundabout, knowing that anyone could still recognize me from behind from my clothes and scarf.

Most of the women in this town wore a chador, the large, long Islamic cover, and they weren't walking in the street at seven a.m. alone.

I walked faster, arriving at the taxi shop and heading inside. A few drivers were sitting around a table, talking. As I entered, one stood up and said, "Hi, do you need a taxi?"

"Hello. Yes, please, to Cisangan," I replied. "Sure, I'm coming."

He quickly exited the shop and pointed toward a black car parked on the street. "You can sit in the car. I will be there in a few seconds."

## Safe at Last

As I sat in the car, I took a deep breath and felt my heart rate finally slowed down. I was safe at last.

He soon came back to the car, and we started driving toward the villa that was two hours away.

I could finally feel a little less anxious. I had the keys to the villa. All I could think of was feeling safe again. I was exhausted, reviewing how everything had happened so fast! All of my poor friends had been arrested. Their parents should know by now. I thought I should tell my mom to let

Maryam's mom know, but then I thought that maybe I should wait for my mom to wake up before calling her and telling her what had happened.

I was worried for Parsa, too. His dad would be so angry with him for this and also for him not being able to go to work. I closed my eyes. I couldn't sleep in the taxi. I was still worried that they would stop us or someone might see and follow me.

We got to the villa, and I paid the taxi driver. Then, we headed toward the villa. As I tried to put the keys in the door, I saw it was open. That scared me so much again!

I was too tired to think rationally, but I wondered whether the villa had been robbed or who could be inside. I was afraid that I wouldn't be safe. I had the keys that no one else was supposed to have.

With these thoughts whizzing around, I entered the front door calmly. Then I saw two of our friends, who were a couple and had come to the party with us. We were all surprised to see each other.

"Sarah, is that you? How did you get out?" they asked, and I asked them the same question.

They pretended they were a married couple and that she was pregnant. They were older than the rest of us, so the committee had let them go. They returned to the villa and got in through the back door. They were Parsa's friends, whom I had met for the first time on that trip.

I told them my story. It was nice not to be alone, although we were all upset and still shocked about what had happened. I called home, talked to my mom, and told her to let Maryam's parents know.

She was extremely worried, but I could hear that she was relieved that at least I was not still in prison. She said they would be coming with my grandpa to their villa the next day, and I should go and stay there with them. My grandpa's villa was an hour away from Parsa's parents'.

I was still anxious to know what could be done for Parsa. I was thinking of him and how he would be so worried now. I was thinking of Maryam and Ana. What a disaster! All of my friends were in prison. What a trip! Why on earth did we even go to that party? I had genuinely been against driving and going there from the start.

I was lonely and scared that night. I called Roozbeh and told him the story, I needed to talk to someone, and he was always confident. He always had great ideas, and Nothing was too dramatic for him. I told him the story and said that Parsa was in prison now.

Obviously, he was upset. He tried to calm me down and said, "Don't worry; he is going to be okay. They'll let them go eventually." Then he asked sarcastically, calling me by my last name, "Are you in love, Tehrani?"

## *Release and Penalty Charge, But What Happens to the Mental Scars?*

The next day, I got into my car that we had thankfully not driven to the party. I stopped by to pick up Hootan's mom, who was one of our friends. Their place was on the way, and we drove together to the town where we had been arrested. I was scared of being seen and recognized, so I dropped his mom at the station and drove around.

All the parents were gathered outside the station. It had already been two days since we had been arrested. We were hoping that they would let everyone else go today.

I kept driving around until Hootan's mom called me on Parsa's cell and asked me to pick her up near the police station. She looked worried and was close to tears.

"What is going on? Will they let them go?" I asked.

"They are taking them to the permanent prison in Babol."

I couldn't believe what I was hearing. "To Babol's prison? But, why? That is where all the criminals are."

There was nothing anyone could do. A decision had been made.

As we stopped on the side of the street and talked about this, we saw that they were directing all of my friends to get on a minibus. That was like a second shock, and I started crying. Hootan's mom was upset, too, and she could barely say anything.

We headed back to the villa. I called my grandparents' villa, and my mom picked up the phone.

"Get your stuff and come here right now. We arrived an hour ago," my mom said.

The couple staying at Parsa's parents' villa had left that morning, so

I was alone. I got my bag, locked the door, tucked the keys under the doormat, and drove toward my grandparents' place.

I was still tired and emotional when I got there. It was nice to have my family around. Once more, I felt safe, although the thought of the committee still wanting me to show up, as I had escaped, or asking anyone about where I stayed at the back of my mind. Also, I felt bad for Parsa; I was unsure what was happening to him.

"Can you go there and see if you can do anything to get them to release him?" I asked my grandpa.

He said, "There is no way they will let anyone go until they are charged in the court and paid their penalties. We would also need a house title deed to release him." Despite saying that, my grandpa went to prison and took the title deed for his villa to try to get him released. I think Parsa's dad had already come from Tehran at the same time to do the same. They asked them to wait until the court date.

Another day passed, and I kept talking to the other parents on the phone to get more information, hoping the judge would let them go.

They set the court date for a week later, right after the New Year holidays. That meant they wanted to keep them in jail until the court date.

We heard they had released Arvin and had released his car. His father had some connections in town that had helped him get out faster and avoid being charged like the others.

Then, the same day, a few parents donated a few sheep for the ceremony of the religious holidays that was being held, so they agreed to release their kids until the court date. Parsa, Maryam, and Ana were released, too. I was so happy, and so were the rest of the parents, to hear that Hootan, Parsa's friend, had asked everyone to go to his villa when they were released. I drove there to meet them.

It was an emotional time for all of us to meet. All the boys had shaved their heads as part of the regulations of going to jail. Parsa seemed calm, though everyone else was still in shock due to what had happened.

We all sat outside around a long table. Some shared their experiences in jail, the people they had seen, and what they had heard. We had a barbecue for lunch that Arvin's parents made, and then everyone said goodbye and agreed they would meet again on the court date.

I went back to my grandparents' villa. We were due to leave for Tehran in a few days.

On the court date, everyone got charged with twenty-two hits with a whip. They were all scared that they would have to actually be whipped, but thankfully, they could buy out with money. So, everyone paid their dues, and the deeds of their houses held by the police were returned to them.

Parsa had made me a memory book in prison and had written me a few letters. It was the first time I had ever been given something like that, and it was so dear to me and made our relationship stronger.

# CHAPTER 20
## Another Relationship

### *Back to Tehran*

Back in Tehran, we had some really nice days after that. It was springtime. Parsa went to work regularly, and I was about to finish university. It was the last term, and I was studying hard to pass all the twenty-four credits for the subjects I had taken. I would still go to Roudehen a few days a week, where my university was.

One day, we went to a friend's house on the eastern side of the town and were passing the highway near where Roozbeh lived. Without thinking, I asked Parsa, "Do you want me to tell you something that will upset you?" I was laughing.

"What?" he replied.

I pointed. "That is where Roozbeh's house is." I was so naïve and not familiar with men's emotions. I didn't think for a second what effect it might have on him.

He didn't say anything but suddenly took the exit from the side of the highway and made a U-turn under the bridge.

"What are you doing?" I asked.

"I'm not going to Payam and Azita's." "I am sorry. I didn't mean to upset you."

He seemed completely certain, and I couldn't convince him anymore. We argued all night as we went back to his home.

Because it was springtime and the weather was good, we barbecued, went to parties, and invited friends to Parsa's small suite.

I didn't enjoy the parties we used to attend in Shemshak anymore. I didn't like the fact that we were up until the morning and going from this house to another chalet or someone else's place with loud music and a crowd that only wanted to party.

I had lost interest in parties, and taking ecstasy didn't appeal to me anymore. Every time we had ecstasy, I was tired, and it took me a couple of days to recover. Besides that, I couldn't longer deal with the fear of facing the committee. After what had happened during the north trip, I was more scared of dealing with the committee for any reason.

## *The Committee Stops the Party*

A few months had passed after the incident in the north. One weekend, we went to another party at Arvin's condo in Shemshak, the same place we had visited the first time. The house was full of people, dark everywhere, and the music was loud. We were within Arvin's small group of close friends who would stay there for the night, but the party continued until the morning.

They shut down the electricity at one stage, as the neighbours complained, but that couldn't stop the party. Everybody was still talking and walking around. One of our friends, Bahram, played the tempo, and many people danced.

I was tired and kind of upset that we couldn't sleep anywhere. There were so many people and no signs of wanting to go home.

Around six a.m., we suddenly heard a loud banging on the door upstairs. They stopped the music suddenly, and everyone went quiet. The committee had come upstairs and was behind the door. Somebody might have complained, but we weren't sure how the committee got in and came up. It was the first time that had happened.

I was so scared. We were all close to going to prison again. Oh my God! I couldn't bear the stress. My heart was pounding.

All these drunk and high people in a small condo were quiet and not moving. We were all praying, but the person on the other side of the door kept banging away. The next thing was that they could break the door. There was no exit from this situation and no way I could run. We were on the tenth floor.

Then and there, I promised myself that this would be the last time I would come to a party like this in Shemshak. I decided it was enough. I didn't want to do this anymore. I was sick of the parties and the scary atmosphere with people who were high and/or drunk. My life was worth more than this. I was better than all this. I had a purpose. I realized I had to figure out what it was and that enough was enough.

We had been going to Shemshak for ten months since I had tried ecstasy for the first time, and I didn't need to be in such a terrible situation scare of the committee anymore.

After almost thirty minutes of them banging loudly on the door, they stopped and left. People started leaving slowly and quietly. We got so lucky this time. They might have felt sorry for us or doubted whether they had come to the right place, as there was barely any noise coming out of the condo.

## Goodbye to Roozbeh

Back in Tehran, Bardia would call me once in a while. I knew he was planning to move to London, where his aunt lived. He told me his aunt was getting him accepted into a university. We hadn't seen each other since I had been with Parsa, though we had talked a few times.

I wasn't really into the details of what he was actually doing and when he was planning to go. I was quite involved with my life and my relationship with Parsa.

One day, he called me and said, "Tehrani"—he always called me by my last name or Bache—"I'm leaving to go to London. Don't you want to see me to say goodbye?"

I was hesitant to see him, as I knew Parsa was suspicious. If he ever found out, our relationship would be over. I was also scared because Parsa checked on me constantly. I wanted to see Roozbeh to say goodbye, but I kept wondering if it would be worth it if Parsa found out.

I decided to go to Roozbeh's house few days later. I was so scared of

Parsa finding out that I looked in the car's rearview mirror while driving to Roozbeh's house to ensure he wasn't following me. When I got there, I was glad to see him.

He excitedly shared some details about his plans with me once he got there, and we chatted as we always do. His mom came to visit him, and I also met her for the first time. She looked just like him. She was nice but serious, yet I felt no discomfort meeting her. I felt sad that he was leaving but happy for him.

I got back, and no one realized I had seen him except Maryam, my best friend, whom I told.

## My Roller Coaster Ride with Parsa

My relationship with Parsa was becoming a roller coaster ride. After the first few months, we argued and fought over unimportant matters. He always seemed to be stressed about something. He had to be at work at certain times, or his dad would get mad. That didn't bother me. But, in general, his overall attitude made me unhappily angry. Maybe I was still rebounding from my relationship with Abtin. I wasn't sure.

Parsa presented himself as a lover who was a deep victim in our relationship, and, of course, I was the evil person and heartless bitch. This was to the extent that my mom would call him "innocent Parsa" jokingly when he called my house and asked my mom if he could speak with me on the phone.

We used to go to a friend's house where their parents were always around and sometimes hung out with us. The father, Farhad, asked me about our relationship one day. He said, "Sarah, what have you done to Parsa that he is so in love with you? He adores you. This is not fair," and then he smiled.

Of course, deep down, I also believed that. I thought he was so in love with me, as he and everybody else had said. But I also knew he was not the person I wanted to spend the rest of my life with. I didn't like his lifestyle. I didn't like the fact that he smoked weed all the time. We had talked so much about it, and he had promised to stop smoking. But he didn't!

He even pretended that he had stopped and went to the gym every day. Then I caught him in his car again, driving close to our house and his workplace, and he was smoking again.

He was also the suspicious type that I couldn't stand. I would get anxious whenever I thought about him checking on me about everything I did. At the same time, we had so much fun with friends. We would go to their houses or gather at Parsa's place.

During the summer, we went to the north a few times. One of the trips was with two other couples and a few friends. He got jealous because I talked to one of the guys "too closely." And, suddenly, he said he had to go downstairs to rest in the studio apartment attached to the villa.

After a while, I checked on him, and he wasn't there. When I called him, he said he was returning to Tehran. I couldn't believe it!

"Tehran?" I exclaimed!

"Yes. You stay there and get cozy with your friends," he said.

"I wasn't even cozy with him. He just talked to me for a minute." I answered.

Parsa didn't say anything and hung up. I was furious.

I returned to my friends and told the couple we were staying with that Parsa had left. Then I decided to go back to Tehran, too. I didn't want to stay there without him. He'd made me feel so guilty, but he wasn't longer answering his phone.

My friends told me, "Don't go back. It isn't safe for you to drive alone all that way."

But I couldn't understand anything else. I was seriously angry and had to talk to him to explain that he was wrong. So, I drove back the five hours alone.

When I got back, Parsa finally answered his phone. I explained that he was wrong and that I had no intention of flirting with the other guy. He told me that I didn't understand. He believd that guy liked me and he was hitting on me.

As much as we had good, romantic times, we fought a lot and argued to the extent that, when my dad was home, he sometimes heard our arguments and fights from downstairs.

My brother, Pouya, who was almost seventeen then, was looking to get a part-time job in the summer. Therefore, I asked Parsa, "Do you guys need help at the store?"

"Yes, we are looking for sales associates."

So, Pouya started working at their clothing shop.

This didn't turn out to have the best outcome in my relationship with Parsa, as Pouya would report all the details about Parsa to my parents, especially since he smoked weed. As it turned out, my dad, who would never acknowledge his existence openly anyway, had quite a negative opinion of him and generally disliked our relationship.

# CHAPTER 21

## Deciding to Leave Iran

### *Hope from London*

One day in the fall, I was on my computer when I suddenly got an MSN messenger alert. When I checked, it was from Roozbeh, who had been in London for a few months now. We chatted, and he said, "Sarah, you should come here. This is another world. It's amazing. Don't waste your time there." He went on and on, telling me about his life, how great his university and life were now, and how interesting London was. I was blown away.

When he was in Iran, we would always talk about leaving and discuss how it would be possible. Now, he told me about the differences he was experiencing, suggesting that he could help me get accepted by a university he had connections with.

I felt a rush of blood as I chatted with him. This was it. This was my way out of this country. I didn't care about anything in my life here. There should be more to life than this.

I hadn't enjoyed going to parties, smoking weed, or taking ecstasy for a long time, and I couldn't trust my relationship with Parsa, either. This was what I had been waiting for, for a long time. I thought to myself, I should talk to my dad to convince him.

I didn't feel anything for Roozbeh, either, but while he was telling me about how amazing the city was and how I should seriously think of moving, at the bottom of my heart, I was happy that he was there. And, of course, the possibility of moving there would make me even happier.

The next day, we were going up north again. This time, I was going with a few friends, without Parsa. We weren't talking at the time because of a fight, so I decided to get away. I couldn't stand his insensitivity and lack of communication. I felt that he was victimizing me, and I couldn't understand what was going on with him. Everything was confusing. But I realized that I didn't want him in my future life, that he wasn't the right person for me!

## *Letter to My Father*

When we got to Shomal, I went upstairs to my room and started writing. I wrote down all my feelings for my dad and how depressed I felt. I also told him how my goals for the future wouldn't be accomplished here. I asked him to help me leave for London to study there and have a different future.

While everyone was partying downstairs, I wrote, crying, trying to describe and share as much as possible with my dad so I could convince him it was right for me to leave. It turned out to be a ten-page letter when it was done.

When I finished, I felt much lighter and couldn't wait to return to Tehran to give it to him. Nothing else was important. It was just about my plans to leave Iran, which had been ongoing since high school. But I had never been so close to that dream becoming a reality.

The day after we returned to Tehran, I left the letter in my dad's briefcase without him noticing. The next day, when he went to work, and I saw that he had found and read the letter. I asked him if he had read the letter when he returned home.

With a smile, he responded, "Yes." He seemed impressed and pleased but hesitant.

That was the best moment I could catch him— when he was impressed with me, my actions, and my decisions. It wasn't easy to impress him. He was a successful businessman who had three published books. He gained a lot of experience by travelling and living around the world. He had sat with and hung out with many people in Iran and other countries and built a successful business himself. He had also provided everything that was best for his family.

He used to tell me that he made money "here," pointing to his brain. Another thing that he'd like to point out was that a man had to have rough hands that worked and weren't manicured and fragile. Only then would he be a real man. He had a much higher IQ than others and could see and feel things from a different angle. And, of course, he talked to me all the time.

Mostly, I didn't enjoy my father's talks because they were always forced on me. I was always on the run and didn't want to confront or communicate with him again. I always had to sit and listen to him talk for hours while he drank a glass of whisky next to him, beside the fireplace. I always wanted to run away. It wasn't just that these talks were long; it was because he tended to get him angry, which was scary.

That night was a little different, although he seemed genuinely impressed and wanted to hear what I had to say, including my plans to move to London. I told him about Roozbeh, and that he had moved there and was studying for his master's degree. He had connections that could help me get university acceptance. My dad listened.

When I finished, he said, "Okay, so ask this guy how he can get these things done, and we'll see."

I was on top of the world! I couldn't believe that he agreed with me going to London, to a new world and country. The future seemed so bright, and the thoughts of leaving Iran were so overwhelming that I could barely sleep that night.

I messaged Roozbeh on MSN to let him know what had happened. He said he had to get my documents and transcripts and the offer letter from the university with which his friend had contacted. Then he would send me a contract and offer letter soon.

At the time, I felt that my life was finally about to change. I was on top of the world and so happy. I was 20 years old and had had to deal with a lot of sorrow and restrictions. I used to cry so much before I went to sleep almost every night.

The crying somehow calmed me down when I couldn't find an answer to my questions, and then it became a habit. When Abtin and I had broken up, and after I had the accident, it seemed that I had grown up somehow and had gotten less emotional, beginning to think more rationally. I still wasn't feeling connected to anything or anyone, though. Not my family, not my boyfriend, and not my friends, or society and people who were around me. However, I was determined to find my purpose and a goal to motivate and challenge me.

I felt that I needed something to look forward to. That felt like what life was all about. It made sense to me that life was about suppression, blame, restrictions, or the other extremes that were common for the people in my age group.

Those parties, taking pills, smoking weed, not sleeping, and dancing until the morning, I couldn't do that, either. It was fun and helped me get along with the pressure of everything in my life for a short time, but it wasn't what I wanted.

## *Light at the End of the Tunnel*

That was it. It was the other extreme to feel relief from the pain of not having the freedom as a girl within those years of my life that, of course, I didn't understand. I only knew that I hadn't found a way of living that felt right to me.

But now, for the first time, I saw a door with a light at the end of the tunnel had opened, and I was ready to do whatever it took to get there.

A few days later, Roozbeh emailed me a file. I had graduated with a BA in English Language Translation, and Dad had been teaching me how to correspond in English, how to start or end emails, etc. I printed out the file, and we read it together. It was a contract with Roozbeh's friend.

As my dad read it and we understood what it meant, I waited for his reaction. He didn't seem against it but said, "Okay, let me think about it."

I got a little uncomfortable because I hoped things would move forward fast. But, of course, this had to follow its own process, like everything in life.

A few days passed. I didn't reply to Roozbeh because I hoped my dad would make a positive decision.

All my thoughts were about this opportunity. I wasn't paying much attention to Parsa or anything else. Everything that used to be important had suddenly become unimportant.

After a few days, my dad came home and said his friends had introduced him to a gentleman who had a connection between universities in England and students. His name was Mr. Asgari, and my dad had his number. He was out of town but would be back in town on Friday. Dad said he planned to call him.

I wasn't expecting this. I thought, So, what about Roozbeh and his friend who is waiting for the contract? But I didn't say anything.

On Friday, we went to our usual family lunch together. Before we left the car, Dad called Mr. Asgari, and they set a time to speak again next Monday.

Dad and Mr. Asgari talked, and he explained the process to Dad. He told him that he could get a conditional offer from the international department of one of the well-known faculties of the University of London: The School of Oriental and African Studies (SOAS).

They would need me to achieve the required minimum International English Language Test Score (IELTS) requirements for me to start the program next September. It was close to the end of the year (December 2001), so I had almost ten months to study and get the needed scores.

I couldn't believe that this was finally happening! At last, I had a clear path of what I could do, and I thanked God for it. I told Roozbeh that my dad had decided to follow this path, he seemed happy and pleased that I'd be moving there, too. We didn't have much contact those days, though. Our only way of communication was via MSN messenger or email.

I focused on taking the IELTS test and started looking for a teacher who could teach me how to do the test and read through the material within a limited time. I booked my first test for February 2002.

Meanwhile, Mr. Asgari sent the paperwork for the conditional offer from the university. I took it to Parsa's house so Mrs. Lia, his mom, could help me fill it out. As I've had mentioned before, she was a native English speaker and was my first English teacher when I was ten.

I was so happy, although the thought of actually studying at a British university was giving me butterflies. I tried not to think about it too much and to focus on studying. I needed to figure out the academic IELTS test.

We rarely went to Shemshak for those parties anymore. We hung out with different groups of people in Tehran. Everything was going well except for the fights I had with Parsa occasionally, which were stressful.

In February, we decided to have a party at his place for my birthday.

We invited some friends, bought food and snacks, and prepared everything.

About twenty people came to Parsa's studio, including his ex-girlfriend with her husband, Maryam, and Ana, and a few of Parsa's other friends, also an old friend who was there with a girl called Arghavan. I didn't know her, but it turned out that she had previously dated our mutual friend.

It was my twenty-first birthday, and Parsa had thrown the party, which was so special for me. When I blew out the candles on my cake, I wished that everything would work out for me, that I go to London to start a new future. I prayed deeply and asked God to make it happen. I felt blessed to be surrounded by good friends and haved a boyfriend who loved me so much, even though we fought so often. I thanked God and asked him to help me with the new life in London.

In March, we went to Shomal for a few days around Iraninan New Year, but Parsa had to be back at work, and I had another IELTS test booked for a month later, so we couldn't stay for more than a few days.

I wanted to pass the test this time and was trying to get well-prepared for it. It was going to be held at the British Council in Tehran. I spent a lot of time studying and didn't spend much time with Parsa, except during the weekends.

One day, he said, "If you're going to leave, what happens to our relationship? Will you marry me?"

I told him, "I don't know. I have no idea what it's like there. I've never been to London. I've never lived there."

The last thing on my mind was getting married at that point. I knew my parents had no thoughts about it, either. Deep down, I knew Parsa wasn't the right person for me.

It seemed he didn't take this conversation easily and couldn't digest what I told him. But we didn't discuss it further.

# CHAPTER 22

## Parsa and the Final Chapter

### *So, This is How You Cheat on Someone*

Parsa had a cell phone, but we still called each other on our landlines, mostly at home. Although, when Parsa was at work, I would call him at the shop. He used to call to see how I was doing, to check on me every couple of hours, and we used to talk. One afternoon, I felt he hadn't called for a few hours and began feeling strange.

It was a strong feeling, somehow, I felt something wasn't right. I called him at his house, but the call went to his answering machine. He didn't answer his cell phone, either. When that happened, I usually said something on the answering machine, and he would pick up the phone. But he didn't, so I left a message.

Then I called the shop, and his mom, Lia, answered with a pleasant tone. I asked if Parsa was there. She replied, "No, Sarah Jan, If you hear from him, please tell him to call me. I need to talk to him, too."

It was even more strange that maybe something was wrong since his mom didn't know where he was. He was usually either at the shop or at home. This couldn't be right.

I grabbed my manteau and scarf in less than a minute and ran toward the door. I don't know why I felt that way or what was happening to me. Maybe, subconsciously, I was aware of what was going on.

I ran to my car, got in, and drove as fast as possible to his house. My heart was pounding so loudly in my chest that I could hear it. My only focus was to get there as soon as I could.

It was unlikely that Parsa wouldn't answer his house phone and not be at work, either. I left onto their street, parked the car, and got out of the car. At the door, I didn't ring his bell, instead, I rang his neighbour's doorbell. They were two brothers to whom Parsa had introduced me. They lived in the condo next to Parsa's studio.

One of the brothers answered, and I said, "Hello, this is Sarah. Could you please open the door?"

Without asking any questions, he opened the door.

I walked along the pathway in the yard where the door to his studio was located. I opened the door and went into the house. Parsa ran out of his bedroom with messy hair and a concerned look. He was more shocked at seeing me there than I was from being there and seeing him in this situation.

"Who is here?" I asked. He didn't reply.

At that point, I felt as if the blood was frozen in my veins. All the small muscles in my face were stuck and barely moving. It felt as if another person had come out of me. I was like a wild tiger who had been wounded by an arrow and was looking to rip someone's chest apart. I knew someone was in the room, but I wanted to hear it from Parsa. However, he wasn't saying much.

Eventually, I went to his bedroom. I couldn't believe what I saw. It was Arghavan, the girl who had come to my birthday party at Parsa's house with another friend. We had seen her a few times, and she'd talked about breathing, meditation exercises, and massage therapy for pain.

She told me that she used to date our mutual friend, Allen. She was sitting on the floor with her head down, holding it. I shouted at her to look at me. She didn't change her position but did look up. Her eyes were so red that I assumed they had been smoking weed right before I got there.

"This guy you see here asked me to marry him a few days ago. In this room, after being in a relationship for almost two years. If you think he is the right guy and a good human being, go for it. He's all yours!"

I was kind of naïve. With my words, I thought I could educate this girl about the kind of person Parsa really was—a cheater. I was also naïve to think that myy words had effect on the girl who knew I was Parsa's

151

girlfriend, was in his room, making out, just a few weeks after we had met at my birthday party at the same house.

As I walked out of the room, I lit up a cigarette and started smoking it. I looked at Parsa, who looked quite ashamed and embarrassed

He shouted at me complainingly, "Yes, I begged you to marry me a few days ago, here in this house, but what was your reply? You said you were not sure right now. You said you wanted to go to London but didn't know about the future."

Looking at him and his desperate face, I laughed hysterically. I picked up another cigarette from the table, lit it, and walked out. I had never been so shocked in my life. He was a person who everyone thought was so much in love with me ... and I did, too!

## The Aftermath of Parsa's Cheating

He looked innocent in our relationship, while I was perceived as the bitch who had him at the tip of my fingers to do anything I wanted.

As the blood in my veins still felt as if it was frozen, I drove to Maryam's house, which was a few streets away from Parsa's. I was trying to process everything that had happened. I rang the bell and said, "Maryam, can I come upstairs? Something crazy just happened."

Ana opened the door with a concerned look and said, "Come in, Maryam. What is going on?"

Their mom and dad were watching TV. As usual, they were nice and greeted me calmly.

We went to her and Maryam's room, and I told them the story. I couldn't cry, but I was still shaking. They brought me one of their dad's beers, and I shared the details. They were in shock, too. Ana was swearing at Parsa and said she knew the bastard wasn't right for me. Maryam was quiet and just looked disappointed about the whole thing. They both insisted I stay longer, but I had to return. I knew that my parents get worried thinking, I should have been at home by then.

I didn't feel good as I drove back home with different thoughts in my mind. I said hello to my parents and went to my room.

That night, and for about two weeks after that, I could barely sleep at night. In the morning, it was hard for me to get out of bed. I didn't know what was happening, but I was tired and heartbroken. The fact that Parsa had seemed so intensely in love with me, and everyone else thought the same way, didn't match what I had witnessed.

My mom would talk to me any chance that she could, trying to explain that my future would be different. She kept reminding me that he wasn't the right guy, which I already knew. Meanwhile, Parsa called more than five times daily, either hanging up or asking my mom to talk with me. When he spoke to my mom; she told him I wasn't feeling good and didn't want to talk.

One day, I remembered a friend of my friend, Parisa, whom I had met a few times. She had told me that whenever she had really bad issues to deal with, she would say her Namaz, the Islamic prayers, and they helped her get along with her life. I decided to start doing that the next day.

After two weeks, I wore the chador and said the morning prayers that I had learned and memorized in high school early in the morning. This was deep meditation and provided me with a connection to God or my inner self that, back then, I wasn't aware of.

That day, I asked God to please help me get over this trauma. I didn't want to be stuck with these awful feelings. After what had happened with Abtin, I was certainly stronger, but I wasn't strong enough to get over this easily.

I said all my prayers that day and found that I could sleep better that night. The next day, after I said prayers, the same thing happened. I felt stronger and stronger, and I gradually got better and better.

## Speaking to Parsa Again and Finally Standing up for Myself

Parsa's mom called to talk to my mom and told her that Parsa was ashamed of what he had done. She said he wanted to apologize and asked my mom to convince me to talk with him. I really couldn't stand the sound of his voice when he called for the hundredth time after two weeks but Mom brought me the phone and asked, "Sarah Jan, it's Parsa. Can you talk to him?"

I reluctantly said, "Okay." I was disgusted to hear about anything he had to say, although, truthfully, a part of me was still curious to know what he had to say.

Would he tell me the truth, or would he deny it? "Sarah," he said with the same innocent victim voice.

Then, without waiting for me to say anything, he started talking. "I swear it's not what you think. Arghavan was here to heal my back, as she is a healer, and her hand energy is very strong. I believed that she could massage me and make me feel better. You know how I've been suffering from back pain since last year. When you came in, we were just looking at the painting on the wall of my room."

I couldn't believe that he was denying everything so easily. Deep inside, although I was furious, I was laughing with anger, thinking how I had caught him with this girl in his bedroom. I saw with my own two eyes that he looked like they had been making out when he had come out of the room. The girl hadn't even defended herself or anything. She wasn't even bringing her head up to look at me. And he was still denying everything that had happened so clearly, trying to make me believe I was wrong.

I was silent, and he kept going on and on.

"A few days ago, in the same room, I begged you to marry me, remember? And your response was that you didn't know. You said you wanted to go to London and decide later and that you weren't ready to get married."

He stopped talking, waiting for me to respond. When I was still silent, he asked, "Isn't that true?"

I responded with, "Parsa, so what? Is this how you thought you loved me, how amazing your love is? Now it's proven to me."

I can't remember how long we talked. At the end of the conversation, he said Arghavan wanted to call me and tell me I was wrong. He insisted that it wasn't how I thought everything had happened and that I was mistaken. I told Parsa I didn't care about what she had to say and hung up.

It had been a mistake to let him talk with me again. I knew it then but still allowed it to happen.

In the meantime, everything about my trip was happening quickly. If my results for my IELTS exam were high enough and ready in time, I would be leaving Tehran for London in September of that year. It was still May, but only a few months were left, and I was excited about it.

Parsa, on the other hand, was making me nervous. We saw each other again. I was getting anxious when I saw him. I couldn't trust him anymore. It seemed to me that he had another character. Still, I was trying hard to convince myself everything was ok. But it was impossible to gain the trust back.

The girl I had seen in his house, and who Parsa had repeatedly promised me was with him to get rid of the back pain, called me the next day with a fearful tone, she said, "Hi, Sarah, this is Arghavan." I couldn't say hi back and just listened. She softly said, "Look, I know you are very upset, but it's not how it seems. I was there to heal him and massage his back. He told me he'd been suffering from back pain for a long time. Nothing happened between us."

I smiled silently. I was so furious. What is she talking about? I thought to myself. I had seen Parsa's face and body when he had walked out of his room. His shirt was on, but everything else had shown what was happening. She was Trying to deny it and helping Parsa with his denial. It was so funny.

"Listen," I told her, "you knew he had a girlfriend and that it was me. You came to my birthday party at his house. To me, a girl who hooks up with a man knowing that he is with another woman is a prostitute." And then I hung up.

I was shaking, but I took a deep breath, satisfied that I had been able to tell her what I wanted to. I was still in disbelief that she had dared to call me.

I saw Parsa a few days later, and we went out for dinner. His soft tone was so deceiving. He seemed to be the most innocent man in the world. He seemed quite ashamed about what had happened and was trying to gain my trust. But it wasn't working. We argued more than before. I would never believe what he told me about his actions or where he was going anymore.

## The Last Fight

A few weeks later, I went to his house one day in June. His friend, Rami, was there, too. We fought about a few things again. I ran toward the door to leave, and he pulled my hand. I got away, went up the stairs, and

155

pushed one of his vases, which dropped on the floor and broke as he chased me toward the house's back door. He kept saying, "Sarah, please stop."

I entered my Nissan Patrol, rolled the window down, and told him, "Please do not call me again."

That day, I'd had a wisdom tooth taken out, and I had stitches in my mouth. As I closed the window, he slapped me through the car window opening hard. I was all fired up and forced the window up. Then I drove over his foot.

I called my friend, Mina, and told her that it tasted as if my mouth was full of blood. I was in tears when I told her what had happened. She told me that she and her husband were at the house of one of their friends and asked me to join them there.

I went there straight away. They had a small gathering with a few other couples who were together, having dinner, when I arrived.

"Sarah," Mina said, "promise me you will forget about this guy and never talk to him again. He is an asshole. He is not the right person for you."

I did listen to Mina, as I needed someone to guide me. I needed someone who would understand and tell me what was right and wrong.

"I promise," I told her, and that was it. I didn't respond to any of Parsa's calls from that day, even though he tried calling many times afterwards.

## Acceptance Spells New Beginnings

I received the acceptance letter from the School of Oriental and African Studies (SOAS) in University of London. I was over the moon. Next, I had to schedule an appointment to go to the embassy and apply for a student visa.

In the meantime, I was anxious and impatiently waiting for the day to go to the embassy with my mom. I still had to wait for a few other documents. Everything had to be translated into English, including my birth certificate, transcripts, and my bachelor's degree, all the docs had to be certified by the Ministry of Education. They told me it would take a few months because they were still processing the students who had graduated the year before me.

Over the next few weeks, I had to go there many times to follow up. My mom was always with me, helping me gather everything they needed.

One night, we were invited to a party in a town close to Tehran called Kordan. I knew the host and some of the guests. Parsa was still calling me, desperate to get back together, but I had decided. He was not the right person for me. I was not experienced enough to recognize this clearly because my emotions still ruled everything. But, this time, I was hurt so much again that even my emotions weren't allowing me to get back with him anymore.

I headed to the party out of town with other friends. I was a little nervous that something could go wrong or that we could get caught by the committee. However, the feeling was more intense because I was in the process of arranging my attendance at the university in London. I didn't want anything to interfere with that.

When we arrived at the party, many of my friends were there, which was nice. Everyone was having fun and drinking, and the music was good. There was a great atmosphere.

As it started to get dark, the music got louder. I danced by myself, so happy that, within a couple of months, I was about to be in a place where my life had a purpose. No matter how things would turn out, I would have the freedom to decide my destiny. Wasn't that amazing?

I thought to myself, "When I go to London, I just want to live life and have to wait to get married and have kids and waiting for my husband to decide for me." I was so happy and excited!

Within the next two months, my mom and I went to the embassy, and I received the visa. We set the date for September 8, 2002. We bought two tickets—one for me and one for my dad. He talked to his friend, who lived in London with his wife and two kids, who said he would pick us up from the airport on that date in London.

That was the end of the final chapter of my life in Iran!

I appreciate what my parents did for me and all the effort they put into talking to me and helping me every day of my life.

Printed in the United States
by Baker & Taylor Publisher Services